Praise for
The World as God's Icon

"The arguments developed by Saint Thomas Aquinas remain not only relevant to the discipline of philosophy, but also decisive in determining how we should think about some of the deep questions of our day. Sebastian Morello has done an excellent job in showing this to be so, and in communicating his passion for a philosophy that remains as relevant today as it has been for seven centuries."—SIR ROGER SCRUTON, former Professor at the University of Buckingham

"This vivid and persuasive account of Aquinas as, importantly, a Platonist, does justice both to the depth and complexity of Thomist metaphysics, and to the place of beauty in religion and in the general theory of value. If Aquinas should no longer be seen as an unqualified defender of Aristotle against Platonism, Morello clearly and eloquently explains why."—THOMAS PINK, Professor of Philosophy at King's College London

"In the face of the vast and awe-inspiring landscape that is the work of Saint Thomas Aquinas, commentators are often reduced to scrabbling in the same small foothills of threadbare and second-hand reductions and clichés. In this bold new book, Sebastian Morello exhorts us instead to stride like giants into the mountains."—FR ANDREW PINSENT, Faculty of Theology and Religion, University of Oxford

"Sebastian Morello engages with a profound question concerning the relationship between beauty in art and belief in God. Important to his thesis is the crucial role of Marsilio Ficino, the pre-eminent teacher at the Medici court in Florence, in transmitting Neoplatonic ideas of beauty (from Saint Augustine, the Church Fathers, and Saint Thomas Aquinas) to the great masters of the Italian Renaissance. This volume is an excellent exploration of the influence of the realist philosophical tradition on the artistic achievements of the Christian West."—GABRIELE FINALDI, Director of the National Gallery, London

"The thought of Thomas Aquinas remains for many the highpoint of medieval Western philosophy's conception of the Creator and the created world. In *The World as God's Icon*, Sebastian Morello shows us just how much Aquinas owed to Plato's understanding of these themes and shows us as well how this can transform our world's vision of the essence of truth, beauty, and the good."—SAMUEL GREGG, Research Director at the Acton Institute and Fellow at the Center for the Study of Law and Religion at Emory University

The World as God's Icon

*Creator and Creation in the
Platonic Thought of Thomas Aquinas*

The World as God's Icon

Creator and Creation in the Platonic Thought of Thomas Aquinas

Sebastian Morello

Foreword by
Ralph Stefan Weir

For information, address:
Angelico Press
169 Monitor St.
Brooklyn, NY 11222
angelicopress.com

ISBN 978-1-62138-638-4 (pbk)
ISBN 978-1-62138-639-1 (cloth)
ISBN 978-1-62138-640-7 (ebook)

Cover Design: Michael Schrauzer
Cover Image: John Constable, *Salisbury Cathedral
from the Meadows*, 1831

Dedication

First to Our Lady, the mother of the Church.
Second to my lady, the mother of my children.

CONTENTS

Foreword

At the start of 2015, Sir (then just 'Professor') Roger Scruton wrote to me and another former student of his to ask that we assist him in establishing a new MA program in philosophy at the University of Buckingham. The program, which continues to flourish, would be distinctive in a number of ways. The cohort would meet regularly in a private dining room at the historic Reform Club on Pall Mall. There, either Scruton or another world-leading philosopher would deliver a talk on one of the central themes of philosophy. This would be followed by discussion over dinner and wine, often continuing late into the night. These meetings would be complemented by one-to-one tutorials and *ad hoc* events, and the course would encourage students to take the wide-ranging and cultivated approach to philosophical enquiry for which its director was well known.

For five years I had the pleasure of assisting in running the MA in Philosophy at Buckingham's Humanities Research Institute, and it was during this period that I came to know the author of this volume. I was fortunate enough to co-supervise, alongside Scruton, Sebastian Morello, in his work on the thought of Thomas Aquinas and the wider classical realist tradition, research to which this book's themes can be traced. It is my very great pleasure to recommend this book and its author, and to offer a few words about the content of the coming pages. Scruton, sadly now deceased, continued to supervise Morello into his doctoral research, and I know that he also held both this book and its author in very high regard.

This volume sets out, in a scholarly but accessible fashion, the participation metaphysics of Thomas Aquinas. It does so in the service of two more specific objectives. First, that of challenging the enduring idea that Aquinas is an exclusively Aristotelian philosopher. And secondly, that of establishing a Platonic aesthetics based upon Thomistic metaphysics. Some comments on the importance of these objectives are appropriate.

There still dominates, among philosophers and readers of philosophy, a perception that Aquinas's system is essentially that of Aristotle, only adjusted to accommodate the ideas of medieval Christianity. This perception is much to be regretted, for it distorts Aquinas's philosophy to its disadvantage. And it encourages the idea that, with little to learn from the most influential thinker of the Middle Ages, students of philosophy may safely skip from Classical Antiquity to Early Modernity without missing much in-between. In contrast, this book presents, with force and lucidity, the case for seeing Aquinas's system as an innovative synthesis of Platonic and Aristotelian ideas whose insight and originality merit its fame and reproach its neglect. Furthermore, Morello places this argument in the context of a wider historiographic lesson. There exists, he observes, a general tendency to view the history of ideas in terms of a "narrative of discontinuity." (This tendency is, I suppose, the natural but unfortunate result of the fact that understanding the history of ideas means drawing distinctions—distinctions which are more easily internalized the more we exaggerate them.) The result is a distorted vision of intellectual history as a sequence of ruptures. This book is a valuable corrective, placing Aquinas's work in a "narrative of continuity" that runs from Ancient Greece to Renaissance Europe and beyond.

That "narrative of continuity" includes, as one of its central strands, the Platonic tradition. Platonism is responsible for many of the most attractive ideas in Western philosophy. Among these is the connection that the Platonists draw between aesthetic and religious experience, and in particular the thesis that we can "rise to the contemplation of the divine through the senses," as Abbot Suger put it. This thesis may not be in step with mainstream philosophical aesthetics today, but that is more due to a conventional antipathy for religious ideas than to any theoretical consideration. For those who take seriously the existence of God, there is well-evidenced intuitive appeal and obvious attractiveness in the idea that we are able to glean some appreciation of the divine nature in the aesthetic experience. It would be a great disappointment if Christianity's greatest philosopher had no place for this idea. And yet, this seems to be true of the exclusively Aristotelian Aquinas of common report. Against this, Morello argues that Aquinas's philosophy may be regarded as articulating a metaphysical foundation for Platonic aesthetics of great sophistication and precision. This will be welcome news for admirers of Aquinas with Platonic sympathies.

The ontological, intellectual, historical, and aesthetic ideas discussed in this book are difficult. Few writers combine the intellectual caliber and authorial flare to communicate them as they are communicated here, in prose that is conversational yet rigorous, vivid yet elevated. Morello has, furthermore, that essential characteristic of a humane philosopher: he really thinks that what he is writing about is important. There is much more work to be done on creatively retrieving Aquinas's philosophy, as well as in its application for the present day. This book is not the last word on this theme, but it is a tremendously valuable work on a topic that merits serious attention.

Dr Ralph Stefan Weir
Lecturer in Philosophy
University of Lincoln

Preface

Glory be to God for dappled things—
    For skies of couple-colour as a brinded cow;
      For rose-moles all in stipple upon trout that swim;
Fresh-firecoal chestnut-falls; finches' wings;
    Landscape plotted and pieced—fold, fallow, and plough;
      And áll trádes, their gear and tackle and trim.

All things counter, original, spare, strange;
    Whatever is fickle, freckled (who knows how?)
      With swift, slow; sweet, sour; adazzle, dim;
He fathers-forth whose beauty is past change:
      Praise him.
        —Gerard Manley Hopkins, *Pied Beauty*

I T IS OF COURSE my hope that this book will be of interest to many. I am however aware that writing it has been for me a way of making explicit, and giving philosophical foundation to, a certain way in which I have always seen the world. From as early as I can remember, I have viewed the world as something both utterly beautiful and yet fallen; a world that aims at revealing some unseen mystery and yet all the while is unable fully to do so. The connection between this "enchanted vision" and the claims of religious traditions became ever more obvious to me, and in my mid- to late teens I spent much time reading books of comparative religion.

Obviously (for I am describing an experience far from unique to me, in which I am sure most of us share) in some moments more than others it was clearer to me that the world ought to be seen like this, and I was fortunate even before my twenties to have travelled through much of

Europe, Africa, and Asia, often witnessing examples of astonishing natural beauty. My family home was in north Buckinghamshire, and it is here that I spent most of my life, and to this area I have returned since marrying and making a family of my own. As a teenager I would often walk a few miles through the fields with my spaniel, stopping regularly to study the barley and wheat, smell the flowers along the hedgerow, taste the berries and chase the butterflies. The world seemed to me—and still does seem to me—an enchanted place, to which the proper response is wonder. My walks would generally break at a particular spot on a hill from which I could look over much of the Aylesbury Vale; if I got the time right, on the horizon I would watch the sunset, and the whole sky blush. Sometimes I would yell out at the landscape: "Who are you!" It seemed to me, albeit without any lucid way of conveying this idea, that "behind" the landscape was One who sought to be revealed through it, but that the world I beheld could do this only in some dim and fragmentary manner.

My family was always one to value the arts, and I grew up in a home where the walls were covered in good pictures, the rooms were pleasingly arranged, and music was taken seriously, although my brother was the only one in the family who was ever truly accomplished with musical instruments. Visits to art exhibitions, and regular encouragement to take beauty seriously, were a part of the domestic culture to which I was accustomed. Later I was educated for the stage at an arts college, and increasingly found the arts in general to bestow meaning in a way nothing else could—apart from perhaps a high Anglican liturgy, the only good liturgy I was ever exposed to as a youngster, which seemed to me merely another great artistic accomplishment, albeit of a category quite removed from the others. In any case, to the degree that the world seemed a dim and fragmented communication of its Source, art seemed a way of redeeming the world, that is, the bringing to perfection of something both wonderful and not fully realized. From all these instances of the beautiful I began to engage with questions of *beauty* itself. The Platonic account of beauty, which has appealed to so many and been so influential on the Western aesthetic canon, rendered clear to me many of the connections I had made for some years without proper reflection.

Toward the end of my teens, whilst travelling in India, I was received into the Catholic Church by French monks at a priory on the outskirts of Pondicherry. These monks belonged to an order particularly devoted to the study of Aristotle and St. Thomas Aquinas. The three months of formation they provided in preparation for my reception into the Catholic Church included an introduction to Thomistic metaphysics, epistemology, and anthropology and moral philosophy, alongside the daily tutorials of theology and Scripture study. It did not go unnoticed that I was deeply Platonist in many of my conclusions, and I have never ceased to be, but rather have sought to synthesize what is true in both Platonism and Aristotelianism, which I now argue is one way to characterize Thomism: a Platonic and Aristotelian synthesis... and a lot more.

For those with some knowledge of the *Existential Thomist* School, it ought not to be a surprise that in the works of the scholars belonging to this movement I found support—as well as reason for ample alteration and development—for much of my general worldview. I first discovered the books of W. Norris Clarke, S.J., and subsequently became interested in Cornelio Fabro, C.P.S. and Louis-Bertrand Geiger,

O.P., and later John F. Wippel and Gregory T. Doolan. Throughout this book I rely heavily on the remarkable work of the scholars here mentioned and owe them a great debt of gratitude. Indeed, until the chapter on aesthetics, little original scholarship will be found herein, but rather only an attempt to present in a single work what I consider to be most important in their labors, at least insofar as they present the world as an *icon of God*.

In the last chapter, I return to the topic with which I was first concerned, and which spurred me on to a deeper metaphysical investigation, namely *beauty*. I argue that the ontology advanced here, which I deem to be Aquinas's own, offers a totally theocentric view of the world. It cuts through the mechanistic, materialistic, disenchanted view of reality which has taken hold of our minds due to the transposing of certain positions from the early "scientific revolution" into areas of inquiry where they do not belong. In turn, the question which follows for me personally, for reasons I have just mentioned in brief, concerns the place of art in the worldview Aquinas gives us.

The reader will note that I introduce a theme at the beginning, which rises to the surface at various points, and was held in mind during the whole process of writing the book; this theme touches more upon the *history* of philosophy than upon pure philosophy. This is the issue of whether we ought to see the Western intellectual tradition as one single organic pursuit of truth, or a sequence of ruptures during which competing paradigms displace each other down the centuries, with each being superseded at the point they degenerate into some decadent caricature of what they used to be. No doubt there is *some* truth in this account, but much untruth too, and I plainly lean toward the view that most moments of pre-atheistic intellectual history presented often as moments of rupture are—on a closer analysis—really moments of synthesis and change of emphasis.

Not only do I deem the narrative of discontinuity view of intellectual history largely untrue in itself, I believe it has as a consequence legitimized as "just the way things are" a *real* discontinuity which characterizes modern intellectual history, in which originality—or what purports to be originality—is held in higher regard than a comprehensive and deep knowledge of the masters down the ages. Joseph de Maistre, whose concerns were similar to mine, though in a very different age, offered the sound and moderate (not a trait for which Maistre is known) advice:

> 1) Not to believe that the ancients, even the most celebrated, were oracles: for they said some very stupid things. 2) Not to reject brusquely their observations under the pretext that they conflict with some of our current ideas; this would be another error perhaps more dangerous than the first.[1]

The glorification of rupture, indeed destruction and desecration, which is so obvious in the sphere of art, music, architecture, etc., typifies also the current processes in the moral and intellectual spheres of the modern world. It is blindingly clear that the course we are on, of losing our civilization, is accelerating to a harrowing pace, and I judge it imperative that we rediscover our identity in the West as heirs to a continuous tradition from which we have tragically departed: wisdom and law, sanctified by the grace-transmit-

[1] Joseph de Maistre, unpublished reading notes, "Philosophie C" (1807), MS, Maistre Archives, Archives Departementales de Savoie, Chambery, 19.

ting mission of Jesus Christ through His Church. This book is a request to not "reject brusquely" the ancients, but rather—in the spirit of Aquinas—to sit at their feet, albeit questioningly. We have largely lost our ability to wonder—in both senses: to be truly amazed and to question properly—and as a consequence we have gone to sleep a grey people in a grey world. This book, then, is a humble invitation to see what things look like outside the Cave.

Acknowledgments

I WOULD LIKE FIRST to thank those authors alive today whom I have not met, as we are divided by the Atlantic Ocean, whose scholarship has been so important in the formation of this book: Gregory T. Doolan, Msgr John F. Wippel, and Edward Feser. I hope one day our paths cross and I am able to thank them in person for their tremendous contributions to Thomistic philosophy, and specifically to my own intellectual journey. I am deeply grateful to my mentor, Sir Roger Scruton, who never made the thought of Aquinas central to his own pursuits, but being a man interested in all things interesting, in the final years of his life encouragingly followed the writing of this work and offered critical remarks along the way. I am unable to offer sufficient thanks to Ralph Weir, who went through every page of the work with a fine-tooth comb, and brought his encyclopedic knowledge and razor sharp analytical precision to every discussion of the text. Peter Kwasniewski's examination of the manuscript was invaluable, and his criticisms and suggestions were gratefully received. He has my most sincere thanks. I am thankful to my friend, Pierpaolo Finaldi; many of the fruits of my conversations with him are scattered throughout the book, just below the surface. I am very grateful to John Riess and the team at Angelico Press for taking on my work and turning it into the book you now hold in your hands. Above all I thank my wife, Iulia, who gave me the time required to write this, supported me, and many times suffered for it.

1

Standing in the Tradition
of Aristotle *and* Plato

Those who think that Aristotle disagrees with Plato disagree with me, who make a concordant philosophy of
both.
— Giovanni Pico della Mirandola,
On Being and the One

*Aquinas's supposed preference for Aristotle and the
rejection of Platonism*

U NTIL RECENTLY the received view has been that the
life and works of Thomas Aquinas (with those of his
teacher, Albertus Magnus) marked a fundamental
shift in the Christian academy, namely, a choice of Aristotle
over Plato, with a following rejection of the rich Platonic tradition which, besides being studied for its own sake, had
informed the theologizing of ecclesiastical scholars since the
Apostolic Age. One may put it in the following way: rather
than understanding Aquinas in the context of a *narrative of
continuity*, the received view is one of a *narrative of discontinuity*. This narrative, which I intend to challenge, one finds
repeatedly disseminated by popular writers, historians, philosophers, and theologians. Before I attempt to challenge this
view, that it may not be thought that I here attack a straw
man, I will give some examples of it, loosely following the
sequence above and beginning with popular works.

13

Pius Cavanagh, O.P.'s biography of Aquinas refers to Thomas's work as one of "Christianizing the philosophy of Aristotle."[1] Chapter 2 of Josef Pieper's popular introduction to
Aquinas, *Guide to Thomas Aquinas*, presents Thomas's thought
as a synthesis of what is contained in the Bible and in Aristotle.[2] Indeed, for Pieper, Aquinas's philosophical and theological worldview can be accounted for by reference to these
two sources, everything else being quite peripheral.

G.K. Chesterton's biography of Aquinas is, again, not a
scholarly work, but was greatly admired by Etienne Gilson
and Jacques Maritain, and referred to by Anton C. Pegis as
"the best introduction to the mind and heart of the Angelic
Doctor."[3] In this very enjoyable biography Aquinas is
described as the antidote to the problem of the "Church
. . . being Platonist," and Chesterton continues on to write in
"praise of the practical value of the Aristotelian Revolution,
and the originality of Aquinas in leading it."[4]

Bertrand Russell, from beyond the Catholic world, so to
speak, also held to the narrative of discontinuity, writing that
until Aquinas:

> Men's notions of Aristotle had been obscured by Neo-
> platonic accretions. He, however, followed the genuine
> Aristotle, and disliked Platonism, even as it appears in

[1] Pius Cavanagh, O.P., *Life of St. Thomas Aquinas* (London: Burns &
Oates, 1890), 48.

[2] Josef Pieper, *Guide to Thomas Aquinas* (San Francisco: Ignatius Press,
1991).

[3] G.K. Chesterton, *Saint Thomas Aquinas* (New York: Doubleday,
2001), iii.

[4] Ibid., 56, 58.

St. Augustine. He succeeded in persuading the Church
that Aristotle's system was to be preferred to Plato's.[5]

Whilst Russell's chapter on Aquinas contains many omissions
and inaccuracies, his book has nonetheless been enormously
influential both in the academy and the popular sphere.

There are a host of other works that advance the same—or
similar—views. Aquinas's work has been described as the
calling into question of the "Platonic theories [that] had hitherto reigned unchallenged."[6] David Chidester describes
Aquinas as one who "elaborated an Aristotelian science of
theology."[7] Although he acknowledges Aquinas's use of
Augustine and Pseudo-Dionysius, Chidester ignores the *central* role of Neoplatonism in his thought, stating that
Aquinas's "method of reasoning depended upon integrating
the philosophy of Aristotle into Christian theology."[8] Also, as
is typical of the popular reception of Aquinas, his Five Ways
are taken by the same author to primarily represent Aquinas's
natural theology.[9] This is a mistake we shall address later in
Chapter 3.

Henry Sire calls the work of both Albertus Magnus and
Aquinas a "choice of Aristotelianism," and while disagreeing
with Russell's judgment that "the substitution of Aristotle for
Plato and St. Augustine was a mistake from the Christian

---

[5] Bertrand Russell, *History of Western Philosophy* (London: Routledge,
1995), 445.

[6] Philip Hughes, *A History of the Church* (London: Sheed & Ward,
1948), 430.

[7] David Chidester, *Christianity* (London: Penguin Books, 2001), 249.

[8] Ibid., 250.

[9] Ibid., 250–51.

point of view," Sire appears to agree entirely with Russell that such a substitution occurred.[10]

Frederick Copleston, S.J., in addressing the question of Aquinas's sources, notes that Thomas "made considerable use of Aristotle," and "adapted from Aristotle what he thought was true and made it his own," being "convinced of the great value and of the potentialities of Aristotelianism as an intellectual instrument."[11] These statements on their own are not untrue, but while giving much attention to the "metaphysical analyses which Aquinas inherited from Aristotle," going as far as to state that Aquinas's "concentration on being considered as existence (as *esse*) set in a new light the world which Aristotle described in his metaphysics," Copleston seems unaware of Aquinas's Neoplatonic influences, which were his primary source for this "concentration on being considered as existence."[12]

Another English Jesuit Thomist, Martin D'Arcy, S.J., begins his work on Aquinas by noting that "the tendency of the Patristic age had been Platonic," after which he states that the "victory of Aristotelianism in the thirteenth century marks the turning point in the history of Christian philosophy . . . accomplished by Albert and St. Thomas."[13] D'Arcy expresses the received narrative of discontinuity succinctly:

[10] Henry Sire, *Phoenix from the Ashes* (Kettering, OH: Angelico Press, 2015), 26.

[11] Frederick Copleston, S.J., *Aquinas* (London: Penguin Books, 1991), 63, 66–67.

[12] Ibid., 83.

[13] M.C. D'Arcy, S.J., *St. Thomas Aquinas* (London: Burns & Oates, 1953), 14–15.

> [Since Aquinas] had the gift of working on a large can-
> vas, and ranged through the whole Universe, invisible
> and visible, from the lowest form of matter to the
> divine being, there can be no surprise that Aristotelian-
> ism became the successful rival of Platonism.[14]

What is surprising about the passage above is that in referring
to Aquinas's triumph over Platonism with his use of Aristotle,
D'Arcy points precisely to that which is most Platonic in the
system of Aquinas, namely the created hierarchy of forms, as
I will explain shortly.

More recently, Anthony Kenny has referred to Aquinas's
"two *Summas*" as a "type of synthesis between Aristotle and
Christianity," and called his thought "Christian Aristotelianism."[15] Again, the Neoplatonic heritage in Aquinas is ignored
in Kenny's popular introduction.

Anthony Towey also overlooks this component of Aquinas,
continuing the narrative of discontinuity:

> The novelty in Thomas' approach was that from his ear-
> liest time in Naples and from studying under Albert in
> Cologne he had been exposed to the newly arrived
> translations of Aristotle into Latin. Hitherto, not least
> through the enormous influence of Augustine, the some-
> what dualistic views of Plato had provided the philo-
> sophical framework for Christian thinking in the West.[16]

Philosophy encyclopedias are generally not informative for
this theme, and in some cases explicitly state the opposite of

---

[14] Ibid., 24.

[15] Anthony Kenny, *Aquinas* (Oxford: Oxford University Press, 1980),
16–17.

[16] Anthony Towey, *An Introduction to Christian Theology* (London:
Bloomsbury T&T Clark, 2013), 225.

what is true. One states that "Aquinas's welcome for Aristotle's natural and metaphysical philosophy scandalized some of his contemporaries. Rejecting Neoplatonism he saw ideas as embodied here and now about us."[17] This is straightforwardly false, for—as we will explore in depth in Chapter 3—Aquinas explicitly advances the Neoplatonic notion of perfect forms and ideas subsisting independently from any extramental presence of forms in the world.[18] The Oxford Companion simply refers to Aquinas's thought as a "system of Christian Aristotelian philosophy," with no indication that this system is a much richer synthesis.[19]

One of the most popular contemporary authorities on Aquinas, Edward Feser, in his introduction to Thomas's philosophy, overlooks Aquinas's *participation* metaphysics, and his section on natural theology only examines the Five Ways.[20] A less introductory work by Feser does recognize that the principles of *act* and *potency* are of considerable importance in Aquinas's metaphysics, but Feser seems unaware that Aquinas's specific application of them is Neoplatonic, and not Aristotelian:

> The Aristotelian theory of actuality and potentiality
> provides the organizing theme, and . . . the rest of the

[17] Thomas Gilby, "Aquinas," in *The Concise Encyclopedia of Western Philosophy & Philosophers*, ed. J. O. Urmson and Jonathan Rée (London: Routledge, 1993), 22.

[18] See Thomas Aquinas, *Summa Theologica* (New York: Benziger, 1948), I, 15, 13.

[19] Alexander Broadie, "Aquinas, St. Thomas," in *The Oxford Companion to Philosophy*, ed. Ted Honderich (New York: Oxford University Press, 1995), 44.

[20] See Edward Feser, *Aquinas* (London: Oneworld Publications, 2009), 62–130.

key elements of Scholastic metaphysics—efficient and final causality, substantial form and prime matter, substance and accident, essence and existence, and so on—follow from it.[21]

As I shall demonstrate later, much of Aquinas's Neoplatonism is articulated in Aristotelian terminology, but so is much of the metaphysics of the Neoplatonists, especially that of Proclus. This makes it no less Neoplatonic in its substantive content. More specifically, Aquinas's Neoplatonic metaphysics of participation is expressed in terms of these Aristotelian principles of act and potency, or more precisely, the limitation of act *by* potency, relating to each other as *esse* to *essentia*. This has misled scholars to believe the doctrine itself is Aristotle's; however, Aristotle specifically rejects any notion of metaphysical participation in perfect transcendental forms.[22] Indeed, for Aristotle, the principles of act and potency have no application—apart from perhaps in some highly analogical sense—beyond the question of the change or motion of individual substances. In turn, Aquinas's application of the Aristotelian terms *act* and *potency*, situated within a participation metaphysics, is extremely un-Aristotelian. Nevertheless, the very renowned Thomist Reginald Garrigou-Lagrange, O.P. fails to see this:

> Aristotle already taught this doctrine. In the first two books of his *Physica* he shows with admirable clearness the truth, at least in the sense world, of this principle.

---

[21] Edward Feser, *Scholastic Metaphysics: A Contemporary Introduction* (Lancaster: Gazelle Books, 2014), 7.

[22] See Aristotle, *Metaphysics* I, chapters 6 and 9, in *The Complete Works of Aristotle: The Revised Oxford Translation*, vol. 1, ed. Jonathan Barnes (Chichester: Princeton University Press, 1984).

Act, he says, is limited and multiplied by potency. Act determines potency, actualizes potency, but is limited by that same potency. . . . Aristotle studied this principle in the sense world. St. Thomas extends the principle, elevates it, sees its consequences, not only in the sense world, but universally, in all orders of being, spiritual as well as corporeal, even in the infinity of God.[23]

A striking passage to be sure, but as W. Norris Clarke, S.J. points out, "neither here nor anywhere else in his [Garrigou-Lagrange's] numerous writings on this doctrine does he ever quote or refer to any precise text where Aristotle himself affirms the limiting role of potency with regard to act."[24] Clarke undertook an examination of the whole of Aristotle to confirm that such a notion of potency and act cannot be found therein.[25] Also, Clarke's own study of ancient through to modern commentaries on Aristotle has proven that no commentator until the twentieth century believed Aristotle to have a notion of potency limiting act, including those commentaries on Aristotle by Aquinas. Had Aquinas received from Aristotle this view of act and potency, by which he articulates his entire metaphysics of *participation*, one would expect him to have attributed it to *the Philosopher*, as he was always ready to do with other doctrines. It seems Garrigou-Lagrange and his contemporaries were reading Aquinas's

---

[23] Reginald Garrigou-Lagrange, O.P., *Reality: A Synthesis of Thomistic Thought* (St. Louis: Herder, 1950), 43–44. Similar affirmations are to be found in Paulo Dezza, S.J., *Metaphysica Generalis* (Rome: n.p., 1945), 124; and in Carlo Giacon, *Atto e Potenza* (Brescia: n.p., 1947), 46.

[24] W. Norris Clarke, S.J., *Explorations in Metaphysics* (Indiana: University of Notre Dame Press, 1994), 67.

[25] Ibid., 68.

Neoplatonism into Aristotle, as if the latter had in fact been a Thomist.

Clarke notes that during the late nineteenth-century Thomistic revival, "it was the Aristotelian facet of St. Thomas's philosophy which was the first to emerge into the limelight and to occupy the attention of Thomistic historians."[26] This historical phenomenon shaped the reading of Aquinas for the next half-century, and it was not until Gilson that the principle of *esse*—the act of existence—was situated as the primary contribution of Aquinas to classical realist philosophy; this principle, which neither Plato nor Aristotle had articulated, was what made possible within Aquinas's synthesis a reconciliation of their principal insights. Gilson unintentionally paved the way for the rediscovery of Aquinas's own Neoplatonism by the next generation of Thomists, whose genesis is with the "participationists," Cornelio Fabro, C.P.S. and Louis-Bertrand Geiger, O.P. (to the work of whom much of Chapter 2 will be devoted). Indeed, this area of Thomistic thought is a comparatively recent development, and only in our own age is reaching beyond the peripheries of the philosophical world and being engaged with in new and exciting ways. It has given rise to the distinct school known as *Existential Thomism*. This was foreseen by Charles A. Hart in the following way:

> Perhaps the most important change in the understanding of the fundamental structure of Thomistic metaphysics in recent times is the recognition of the primacy of the decidedly Neoplatonic influence in the formation of that fundamental structure as opposed to the traditional view that Aristotelian influences were

---

[26] Ibid., 89.

the most important. I refer, of course, to the Neoplatonic doctrine of participation. . . . This view of
Thomism with participation as the center doctrine
would make that system primarily radically revised Platonism expressed in Aristotelian notions of potency
and act with an extension of the meaning of these latter
notions which is not found in Aristotle but is original
with St. Thomas. In this light we would consider the
metaphysics of St. Thomas to be a highly original synthesis with Platonic influence superseding that of Aristotle in view of the central character of the doctrine of
participation for St. Thomas.[27]

The success of this philosophical movement—which will
be discussed in greater depth shortly—is evidenced by the
fact that now some authors outside the current are taking
note of the recovery of Aquinas's Neoplatonism. David Luscombe, for example, notes that Aquinas "accepted the Platonic theory of forms and ideas . . . in the mind of God."[28]
However, other scholars of intellectual history are skeptical
of this Neoplatonic recovery within Thomism. Richard
Cross acknowledges that it is "fashionable today to empha-
size Platonic elements in Aquinas's thought, partly as a
response to stress placed on Aquinas's Aristotelianism in the
first two-thirds of the twentieth century."[29] Cross, however,
judges that "this modern emphasis on Aquinas's Platonism

[27] Quoted in Clarke, *Explorations*, 65. The ideas here are developed in
Charles A. Hart, "Twenty-five Years of Thomism," *New Scholasticism* 25
(1951): 3–45.

[28] David Luscombe, *Medieval Thought* (Oxford: Oxford University
Press, 1997), 102.

[29] Richard Cross, *The Medieval Christian Philosophers: An Introduction*
(London: I. B. Tauris, 2014), 106.

misses what is really distinctive about Aquinas."[30] On the other hand, Cross's view may be based on a misunderstanding, for in his own examination of Aquinas's use of the terms *act* and *potency* he concludes that the Thomist application of these terms differs from that of Aristotle, but fails to trace this discrepancy to Aquinas's Platonism, which surely can, in fact, be called a component of what is "distinctive" about Thomas.

The Neoplatonic tradition to which Aquinas was heir

In this book I intend to argue in support of the recovery of the Neoplatonic component in the thought of Aquinas, on the grounds of the indispensable theoretical role this component plays. In the next chapter I will attempt to reconstruct the philosophical role of Neoplatonism in the Thomistic synthesis, with a view to situating the notion of *participation* at the heart of Aquinas's metaphysics. By doing this I hope to show that his worldview is profoundly Neoplatonic, perhaps just as much as it is Aristotelian, although predominantly (but not solely) expressed in the terminology of the latter tradition. Before undertaking this task, however, I will give a brief overview of the history of the notion of participation, whose role in Aquinas's thought is so challenging to the narrative of discontinuity.

That Aquinas marks a triumph over Platonism with his use of Aristotle was a view seriously weakened in the twentieth century first by Fabro and Geiger in Europe, and soon after by Clarke and others in North America. Having begun to uncover the Neoplatonic currents in Aquinas, a new narrative emerged. In turn, Aquinas is now increasingly viewed,

---

[30] Ibid.

by those with a deeper interest in his thought, not simply as someone engaged in "Christianizing the philosophy of Aristotle" (to quote the first example I offered in the previous section), but rather as an heir to the great Hellenistic worldviews of both Aristotle *and* Plato. According to this narrative, having established a highly original and elegant synthesis of these two traditions, he assumed this into his theology; the synthesis itself however belongs first to the order of "unaided reason," that is, philosophy. In any case, as Clarke notes, "it is no longer possible . . . to evaluate the philosophical contribution of St. Thomas—as some of the most distinguished modern historians of Thomism have done—as a decisive option for Aristotle against Platonism."[31]

As stated, the backbone of this synthesis is the Neoplatonic notion of *participation*, on which the next chapter will exclusively focus. The reconciliation of Aristotelianism and Platonism in the Thomistic ontology is made possible by the metaphysical principle of *esse*, a principle—as we have said—absent in the thought of both antecedent traditions. *Esse* is the heart of Aquinas's own contribution to the classical realist tradition of the Schoolmen.

Before, then, attempting in the next chapter to reconstruct this ontology of participation—drawing on primary texts as well as the work of the "participationist" scholars named above—to situate it within Thomism, we will consider a little further the narrative of continuity as it has emerged in the course of recovering Aquinas's Neoplatonism. Having done this we shall, it is hoped, be in a position to make any considerations of history quite secondary to

---

[31] Clarke, *Explorations*, 82.

24

our inquiry, and henceforth primarily engage with what is meant *per se* by "participation metaphysics."[32]

The general meaning of participation in Aquinas is continuous with that found throughout the Hellenistic philosophical tradition, namely rendering intelligible the relationship of the *many* to the *one*, i.e., explaining the common possession, in many subjects, of a given attribute by reference to a transcendent source, whose perfection they receive in part. Another way to say this, for several ancient thinkers, is that that which is finite possesses according to its own finitude that which is of itself infinite. In turn, the question is one of the nature of the finite and the infinite.

The idea of the *infinite* in Western thought may be traced back to Anaximander:

> The Non-Limited is the original material of existing things; further, the source from which existing things derive their existence is also that to which they return at their destruction, according to necessity. . . .[33]

It is difficult to know with what Anaximander identifies the "Non-Limited" (*to apeiron*); perhaps a transcendent divinity, but this is unlikely due to the general proclivity of the Pre-Socratics to posit purely material categories. It is perhaps this tendency which causes Anaximander's Pre-Socratic successors to identify "the infinite with the indeterminate, formless substratum or raw material of the universe, the primeval chaos of matter itself, as yet unperfected by the limit of

---

[32] I am deeply indebted to Clarke's essay entitled "The Limitation of Act by Potency in St. Thomas: Aristotelianism or Neoplatonism?" (ibid., 65–88) for the following historical sketch.

[33] Kathleen Freeman, *Ancilla to the Pre-Socratics* (Cambridge, MA: Harvard University Press, 1948), 19.

form."[34] Antithetical to this is the perfected cosmos, which is seen to be unfolding as matter takes form and is in turn limited, and therefore rendered intelligible.

The next great contribution to reflection upon the notions of the infinite and the finite is to be found with the Pythagoreans. They held that all reality was composed of two opposing forces: the principle of perfection, which was also the principle of *limitation*, identified with odd numbers, music, masculinity, light, etc.; and against this the principle of imperfection, also the principle of *unrestriction*, identified with even numbers, vice, the feminine, darkness, etc. In keeping with general Pre-Socratic materialism, the universe would reach its perfection when it could evolve no more, i.e., when it finds itself permanently limited, the infinitude of formless space having been restricted by intelligible form.

Parmenides is the first to break out of the materialist paradigm; he in turn asks in his own way one of the most fundamental philosophical questions: *what is being?* For Parmenides, *being* is perfect, and we can speak of *being* because it is a *single thing* which can be known by the mind, and therefore must in some way be *limited*. Heraclitus too, as well as the Atomists, all coming after Parmenides, identified perfection with limitation.[35] Although the Pre-Socratics continuously struggled to free themselves from materialist presuppositions and extrapolations, they nevertheless set in motion a tradition of inquiry which has dominated philosophy ever since, namely, that of the relationship of the one to the many, the infinite to the finite, the necessary to the contingent, and the perennial to the becoming.

---

[34] Clarke, *Explorations*, 69.
[35] Ibid., 70.

Plato takes up this current and develops it: "whatever is said to be consists of one and many, having in its nature limit and unlimitedness."[36] For Plato, all things below the Good are a "mixture" of two opposing principles, the infinite being identified again with formlessness, indetermination, and chaos; and the finite, identified with form, intelligibility, and being.[37] According to Clarke, out of this arises the Platonic theory of participation in its embryonic stage:

> In the Platonic framework it is participation in the idea of being which makes a particular idea to be precisely what it is, i.e., this particular well-defined essence. It is participation in non-being or otherness which, by negating the indeterminate or infinite multitude of all other ideas, preserves this particular essence distinct from all others and prevents it from melting into them in a blur of unintelligible confusion.[38]

Plato, then, identifies *limit* with *being*, and *infinity* with *non-being*—a judgment which will later be completely reversed by Thomistic metaphysics.

When treating of the question of the finite and the infinite, Aristotle begins by undertaking a rigorous analysis of all pre-

---

[36] Plato, *Philebus*, 16c, trans. Dorothea Frede (Indianapolis: Hackett Publishing Company, 1993).

[37] The main sources for this interpretation are the following: *Philebus*, 16–18; 23c–30; 61–67; *Statesman*, in *Plato: Complete Works*, ed. John M. Cooper (Indianapolis: Hackett Publishing Company, 1997), 283b–285a; *Laws* IV, 716c. The integration of these two theories of Plato—the theory of ideas and the theory of the finite and the infinite—into a synthesis is indicated clearly in the *Sophist*, 256e, but was not fully worked out, it seems, until the later oral teaching as reported by Aristotle, e.g., in *Metaphysics*, I.6, 9; XIII.4, 5, 9.

[38] Clarke, *Explorations*, 71.

vious Hellenistic thinkers of significance.[39] Aristotle finds
himself in agreement with his predecessors in philosophy
insofar as he takes the notion of the infinite to entail incom-
pleteness and indetermination, to be indefinite, and hence
imperfect.[40] For Aristotle something is perfect when it has
reached its proper finality, that is, it is complete, finished, has
attained its *end*; and Aristotle says that an *end* is a limit.[41]
Indeed, the words *perfect* and *end* even have the same etymo-
logical root in Greek: *teleios* = perfect; *telos* = end.

When Aristotle, then, comes to apply his principles of act
and potency to the composition of form and matter, he
explains that form, or act, imposes limitation on the formless infinity of matter, and thus renders it intelligible.[42] This
is, as we shall see, a conception of these principles quite at
odds with that advanced by Aquinas, who will partly reverse
the matter-form relation so that the former also limits the
latter. [43] As we shall see, this development of Aquinas is possible only within a participation ontology of the kind Aristotle explicitly rejected, i.e., of forms subsisting either
perfectly and separately (as in the Platonic worldview), or in
the mind of God (Aquinas's view).

One may object that Aristotle implicitly posits a kind of
participation metaphysics, insofar as he holds that forms are
in themselves singular and unique, and multiplied only by

[39] *Physics* III.4–8; *Metaphysics* XI.10.
[40] Clarke, *Explorations*, 72.
[41] *Physics* III.6, 207a14.
[42] *Physics* III.6, 207a30–37.
[43] *Summa Theo.* I, 7, 1–2; III, 10, 3 ad 1. See also Thomas Aquinas,
Quaestiones de quodlibet (Leuven: Leuven University Press, 1987), III, 2,
3: "Just as matter without form has the note of infinity, so too form without matter."

reception in matter. However, it would be a huge and quite unfounded leap to assume that Aristotle believed this multiplication arose from the limitation by matter of a form which independently could be called *infinite*. Rather, in explicit opposition to Plato, Aristotle holds that every form is received whole, entire, and equally in every given individual substance of the species.[44] For Aristotle, form is fully determined in itself, and then "stamped successively on various portions of an amorphous raw material."[45] According to this model, material multiplication of a species seems to imply more "an expansion than a limitation of the form."[46]

Aristotle, like the Pre-Socratics, holds that the degree to which a thing lacks limit is the degree to which it lacks substance, and so is further along the chain of being toward the infinite chaos of formless matter.[47] It should be quite obvious, from this point alone, that Aquinas could not, and therefore *did* not, adopt intact Aristotle's ontology:

> Substantial infinity would simply have no meaning in this Aristotelian universe; there is no ultimate common perfection deeper than form, such as existence for St. Thomas, in which the hierarchy of forms could participate according to different degrees or limits. Each form is an ultimate and an absolute in its own right. Correspondingly potency can have no connotation of

---

[44] *Categories* 5, 3b–4a.

[45] Clarke, *Explorations*, 74.

[46] Ibid., 74.

[47] "Perfection is equated with finitude and coincides with form. This philosophy of act does not lead in the direction of the omnipotent Christian God." Joseph Owens, *The Doctrine of Being in the Aristotelian Metaphysics* (Toronto: Pontifical Institute of Mediaeval Studies, 1951), 297.

limiting a plenitude which would be found elsewhere in a higher degree.[48]

Half a millennium after Aristotle, there appeared with Neoplatonism, for the first time in Western thought, a doctrine of participation linked with "a wholly new concept of the infinite and the finite, correlated now with the perfect and the imperfect respectively in a complete reversal of the age-old classical Greek tradition."[49] From the biblical perspective it had not been obvious to contemporary Christians that God should be identified with the infinite. The first Christian academy of philosophy, known as the *Catechetical School*—based in Alexandria, and led by the classical Platonists Clement and Origen—held to the conventional Platonic position that God and His divine attributes could not be called infinite, for then, as Origen argues, He (and His attributes) would be unintelligible, even to Himself.[50] Identifying God with the infinite—which would ultimately be the way by which Christians would defend the absolute transcendence of God against future heresies, all the way up to Averroism in the Middle Ages, and even modern-day pantheistic New Ageism—entered Christianity from without, namely by way of Neoplatonism.

Plotinus taught that form—a perfecting principle of limitation—was imposed on the infinity of matter; in turn, he preserved the old Greek notion of limited, intelligible essences. However, their relation to the divine *One* by "emanation" introduced a new idea regarding the function of

[48] Clarke, *Explorations*, 74–75.

[49] Ibid., 75.

[50] Origen, *De Principiis*, II, 9, in *On First Principles*, trans. John Behr (Oxford: Oxford University Press, 2017).

form, i.e., this principle of limitation limits what is above as well as what is below it. Clarke explains this in the following way:

> All the intelligible essences below the One now appear as limited and hence imperfect participations of this supremely perfect and absolutely simple first principle, which somehow embraces within itself the perfection of all the lower determinate essences but is none of them in particular. The One, therefore, must be above all particular intelligible determination or essence, and can be described only as a supreme indetermination or infinity, not of defect but of excess. Forced to invent a new terminology, Plotinus for the first time in western thought uses the old Greek word for the infinite, *apeiron*, to express this radically new content of indetermination as identified with the plenitude of perfection of an unparticipated source compared to the limited participations below it.[51]

It is commonly accepted that early Christians soon judged that Plotinus and his disciples—a group hostile to the Church—were, unaided by revelation, discovering the Divine Logos itself. By the time of Augustine or Pseudo-Dionysius the influence of Neoplatonism on Christian thought is indisputable. On reading Plotinus one discovers therein the seed of an idea that would be central to Aquinas's metaphysics: a perfection cannot be limited except by something else.[52]

---

[51] Clarke, *Explorations*, 76–77.
[52] See Plotinus, *The Enneads*, trans. Stephen Mackenna (London: Faber and Faber, 1956), V, 5, 6; V, 5, 10–11; VI, 7, 18.

The reception of Neoplatonism by Aquinas

In this section I will spell out the history of Aquinas's reception of Neoplatonism as viewed by Clarke, as well as the other "participationists" broadly speaking, and following this I will move on to a philosophical examination of these views. Aquinas is not in *complete* agreement with Plotinus; the latter, following Plato, still identifies *being* with limited essence, and so places the *One* above being and intelligibility, for he holds the *One* to be unlimited. The notion here is that the intelligibility of a thing is grasped via its *form*. To know what comprises a thing is not enough; one must know its *form*. For example, to speak of a slow-moving wooden shaft is quite different from speaking of a *tree*, for the former merely describes the thing encountered, whereas the latter names the form, and places it in a category shared by others. The form limits the matter to *this* particular thing, which can in turn be known, and therefore the form is considered the principle of limitation. Hence, since the *One* is judged to be unlimited, it must be formless, and therefore cannot itself be intelligible, according to Plotinus. The divine, then, ultimately remains inherently unknowable. Aquinas, as we have said, offers a way around this outcome by introducing the principle of *esse*.[53]

The basic Plotinian ontology centered on an infinite source of all reality, with that reality as a "ladder of being" participating in this source, was systematized by Proclus in *The Ele-*

---

[53] *Esse* is the "act of existence" of any real thing. We can say both *what* something is (*essentia*), and *that* something is (*esse*). Something that comes into existence neither creates itself nor continues to exist inevitably, and therefore its existence is an act which requires philosophical explanation.

ments of Theology, of which we find a "thinly veiled Christian adaptation" in the works of Pseudo-Dionysius.[54] By the Middle Ages it had long been believed that the *Liber de Causis* was a work by Aristotle, but it was proved by Aquinas to have been a summary or abridgement of Proclus's *Elements*.[55] This work, along with the works of Pseudo-Dionysius, gave Aquinas access to the whole system and structure of Neoplatonic metaphysics.

From Neoplatonism the medievals inherited the view that every pure (that is, *unparticipated*) form is infinite.[56] In turn, every finite substance must be a composite of form and a limiting subject. This is exactly the view advanced by Boethius in his short work *De Hebdomadibus*, on which Aquinas wrote a commentary. This position was adopted almost intact by the Franciscan scholastics, who taught that *all* contingent reality was some composition of form and matter, leading to an

[54] Clarke, *Explorations*, 78.

[55] "Thus we find a collection of writings on first principles that are divided into different propositions, in a way similar to the procedure of those examining certain truths one at a time. And in Greek we find handed down a book of this type by the Platonist Proclus, which contains two hundred and eleven propositions and is entitled *The Elements of Theology*. And in Arabic we find the present book which is called *On Causes* among Latin readers, [a work] known to have been translated from Arabic and not [known] to be extant at all in Greek. Thus, it seems that one of the Arab philosophers excerpted it from this book by Proclus, especially since everything in it is contained much more fully and more diffusely in that of Proclus." Thomas Aquinas, *Commentary on the Liber de Causis*, trans. Vincent A. Guagliardo, O.P., Charles R. Hess, O.P., and Richard C. Taylor (Washington: Catholic University of America Press, 1996), 4.

[56] By "pure"—or "unparticipated"—form, I mean a form which is not a correlative principle with that of *matter* in a composition comprising a single substance, but rather a perfect form such as those of Plato's "world of Forms," or the ideas in the mind of God.

early type of materialism. The same view was adopted by Aquinas, but he transformed it "in a highly original stroke of genius, so that the ultimate perfection now becomes the 'quasi-form' of *esse*, the act of existence, instead of form-essence, and the latter becomes itself the limiting, participating principle."[57] Aquinas radically develops the notion of metaphysical participation, whilst—at chapter V of *De Ente et Essentia*—explicitly recognizing its Neoplatonic parentage.[58]

Aristotle had taught that change, or motion, could be rendered intelligible by reference to the principles of *act* and *potency*. Things are composites of act and potency, and certain causes allow for the actuating of certain potencies. The potency of a thing, then, is *really* part of the thing, but is not itself *real*; a more precise way to say this is, the potency of a thing exists, but is not *actual*. For example, an acorn is *actually* an acorn, and only *potentially* an oak, and while it remains an acorn there is no existent oak. Aristotle's doctrine of act and potency is a powerful tool for explaining the nature of change. However, Aristotle applies the doctrine exclusively to this topic. This may plausibly be seen as a shortcoming. Aquinas argues—convincingly I shall claim— that it can be applied more broadly "to express a structure of metaphysical composition within a being, while at the same time safeguarding the intrinsic unity of the composite resulting from the union of two incomplete, correlative principles."[59] For Aquinas, Neoplatonism's weakness on the other hand was its unexplained, and therefore ambiguous, concep-

---

[57] Clarke, *Explorations*, 79.

[58] See Thomas Aquinas, *On Being and Essence*, trans. Armand Maurer (Toronto: Pontifical Institute of Mediaeval Studies, 1968).

[59] Clarke, *Explorations*, 79.

tion of individual substances: from what did they result? What was the specific relationship of the participant to the thing it participates in (henceforth "the participated")? Seeing that the strength of each ontology remedied the weakness of the other, he established an original synthesis, condensed in the oft-repeated formula: *act is not limited except by reception in a distinct potency.* He transformed the meaning of act and potency by situating them within the Neoplatonic participation-limitation framework. Now these principles would be applied to express the fundamental hierarchic structure of the cosmos, i.e., the relation of individual substances to "a first Source conceived at once as exemplary, efficient, and final cause of all."[60]

Aquinas seems to have been quite conscious of his sources, and what he was doing with them. Supporting this surmise is the fact that all of Aquinas's early works express the principle of limitation not in Aristotelian *act-potency* terms, but always in its traditional Neoplatonic terminology, e.g., "Every abstract or separated form is infinite." It is not until as late in his career as the writing of the *Summa Contra Gentiles* (written 1259–1265) that Aquinas begins to express this component of his metaphysics in Aristotelian terminology. By 1271 we have a clear synthesis of the Aristotelian *act-potency* and Neoplatonic *participation* ontologies in a single metaphysical theory:

> Every created substance is composed of potency and act. For it is manifest that only God is his own act of existence, as though essentially existing, insofar, that is, as his act of existence (*suum esse*) is his substance. And this can be said of no other being: subsistent existence can be only one. It is therefore necessary that any other

[60] Ibid., 79.

thing be a being by participation, such that in it the substance participating existence is other than the existence itself that is participated. But every participant is related to what it participates as potency and act, that is, of that which is and its act of existence.[61]

Aquinas, then, is "the first thinker in Western philosophy to be able to effectuate a successful synthesis of the two basic insights of the Aristotelian and Neoplatonic traditions and thus to fuse into one the best elements of the two main streams of Western philosophical thought."[62]

Having offered a brief historical sketch, we are now in a position to look, in much greater depth, at the place of participation in the thought of Aquinas, henceforth in a properly philosophical manner, and only secondarily from the perspective of intellectual history. What follows is my attempt to reconstruct the metaphysical role of participation in Aquinas's thought, in the hope of demonstrating that inasmuch as Aquinas can be said to be an Aristotelian he can also be said to be a Neoplatonist.

---

[61] *Quodlibet* III, 8, 20.

[62] Clarke, *Explorations*, 82.

2

Aquinas and Participation Metaphysics

Consequently, God is being itself, the one itself, the good itself, and likewise truth itself.
——Giovanni Pico della Mirandola,
On Being and the One

The problem of the one and the many

ABOVE I QUOTED PLATO in his reference to the problem of "the one and the many"; for it is this mystery which gives rise to the notion of participation. *Unity* is the necessary property of any real being: for a substance to be what it is, namely a *subsisting individual*, it must be unified. There may be a multiplicity of parts and components within the being in question, but this is possible precisely because its unity is logically prior to the parts and components, and the latter depend upon the former. This, we can say, is a description of the *problem of the one and the many* within a single being. We can extend this same problem to the whole cosmos of real beings: how is it possible that all beings, in relation to each other, are many, and yet share in the common attribute of actual existence? One of the axioms attributed to the fourth-century BC Taoist philosopher Zhuang Zhou is, "Great thinking sees all as One; small thinking breaks down into the many." For Aquinas, the real achievement is to think both together; in turn, this section will attempt to explain how we might maintain that reality is both one and many.

The problem of the one and the many has been called "the ultimate paradox of being and the deepest and most fundamental problem of all metaphysics."[1] To say "this is" of something is to affirm both its difference and its similarity to everything else in reality. In saying "this," we distinguish "this" from "that," and so mark its difference; but in saying "is," we judge it to be real, and so relate it to everything which shares in existence, i.e., all existent reality. One way around this paradox is proposed by Parmenides: to reject the apparent multiplicity as a mere appearance, treating oneness as the ultimate metaphysical state of affairs. The problem with this view is that it requires us to withdraw all our credence in the sensory evidence of multiplicity. This is highly counter-intuitive, and makes subsequent metaphysical speculation extremely problematic (it is difficult to see how relative trust in sense experience is not a fundamental prerequisite for any subsequent metaphysical conclusion). I therefore assume that we should take seriously both the multiplicity and the oneness of being.

Taking seriously both aspects, we must venture out to see how the one and the many might be reconciled at both the micro level of the integrity of each individual substance, and at the macro level of the diversity and unity of all reality. Both Parmenidean radical monism (shared also by the Vedanta school of Hinduism, which looks to the non-dualist Upanishads over other Vedic texts) and radical pluralism (of,

---

[1] W. Norris Clarke, S.J., *The One and the Many* (Indiana: University of Notre Dame Press, 2001), 72.

say, the British empiricists) are rejected from the outset by the Thomist on the grounds that the philosophical explanation on offer eliminates the very data of experience it is supposed to explain.[2]

As stated, any real being is like any other in that it *is*; and yet unlike every other in that it is *this*, and not *that*, real being. For the Thomist, this means that every real being is:

> made up of an inner metaphysical composition or sub-structure of two really distinct, i.e., objectively irre-ducible (not separable), metaphysical co-principles (i.e., roots, or grounds, or sources: "a principle" is that from which something flows, either in thought or in being): one the *principle of similarity*, the other the *principle of dissimilarity*.[3]

---

[2] David Hume, for example, rejects the existence of any necessary connections between distinct beings, including causal relations understood as something beyond mere conjunction. This gives rise to a view of the universe as simply a collection of unrelated objects, about which we can say little. Instead of a formed world disclosing itself to the mind, and the mind representing the world at an epistemic distance, in turn seeing the world via its ideas, it is rather our ideas that are the principles of unity, and there is little to indicate that these correspond to any external reality. Kenny explains: "It is not our inference that depends on the necessary connection between cause and effect, but the necessary connection that depends on the inference we draw from one to the other. Our belief in necessary connection is not a matter of reasoning, but of custom; and to wean us from the contrary doctrine Hume presents his own analysis of the relationship between reason and belief." Anthony Kenny, *A New History of Western Philosophy* (Oxford: Oxford University Press, 2010), 563–64.

[3] Clarke, *The One and the Many*, 80–81.

Similarity and dissimilarity are opposites, and in turn irreducible to each other; otherwise a real being would be unlike every other for the precise reason that it is like them. This is the same as arguing that because Socrates exists, all that exists is Socrates. If we are to avoid this monism, we must insist that every real being has "its own distinguishing note in addition to the act of existence; otherwise, it will coincide with some other member."[4]

Within a single individual substance the relationship between the two distinct principles of similarity and dissimilarity cannot be one of two complete beings, for—as we have said—something is a single substance due to its unity. In turn, the relationship is judged to be that of two mutually correlative co-principles, incomplete by themselves, "within the enveloping unity of the one complete being."[5] This composition is *real*, because these principles are contrary, and therefore irreducible to each other.

The name given by Aquinas to the principle of similarity is "the act of existence" (*esse*), and to the principle of dissimilarity, "essence" (*essentia*).[6] We can call the former a *positive* principle, for it is the basic perfection of all that is real.[7] However, essence, it seems, cannot be a positive principle in this way, i.e., something real in its own right added on to existence, for then it would already have existence within it (otherwise nothing real would be added at all), and therefore

---

[4] Ibid., 81.

[5] Ibid., 82.

[6] These correspond respectively to the predicative and the existential use of the copula "is."

[7] By "basic perfection" I mean the minimal perfection (or completeness) that something needs to be part of reality.

in no way differ from the compositions which constitute the world.[8]

Existence is clearly the basic perfection of any real being, but it cannot be a *minimum*, so to speak, onto which more reality is added, for beyond existence there is nothing; in turn, existence must be understood within the Thomistic ontology as a *maximum*, "an all-encompassing plenitude."[9] *Essence*, then, may be described as the *negative* principle, which limits and diversifies the fullness of existence, partially negating its plenitude to produce every instance of existent reality, and so establish the "ladder of being" which we behold:

> The relations of essence to existence can thus be only one of subtraction, not addition: Existence – essence 1, – essence 2, etc., each of which is a distinct partial negation of the total fullness of existence possible. Essences are thus not something positive added on to a minimum base of existence, but rather intrinsic limiting or restrictive principles particularizing and finitizing each act of existence that is not the total plenitude of pure unrestricted existence, thus allowing for many different real beings, all limited participations, through different essences, in the unlimited fullness of existence itself.[10]

To be clear, by "negative principle" I mean that *essence* is a determinate capacity for limiting *existence*; not quantitatively,

---

[8] The idea of a "positive principle" and "negative principle" is exactly what is entailed by the terms *act* and *potency*. For this reason, as we have seen, and as we shall go on to see in greater depth, Aquinas applies these (Aristotelian) terms to convey the relationship of *esse* to *essentia* in the (Neoplatonic) hierarchy of contingent being.

[9] Clarke, *The One and the Many*, 83.

[10] Ibid., 83.

but qualitatively. It is a receptive principle that holds existence to *this* level on the ladder of being; having no independent reality of its own, "it is totally correlative to the
actuality of existence that fills it."[11] "Receptive" does not
here imply "pre-existing"; rather only that these principles
correlate as negative, receptive, passive principle and positive, *active* principle. The Thomistic solution to the problem
of the one and the many is not the denial of the former or latter—which I have suggested would be no solution at all—
but the metaphysical doctrine of *esse* and *essentia*, comprising
therefore an ontology not of denying, but of reconciling, the
one and the many.

The meaning of participation in Aquinas

I began this second chapter with a brief reflection on the
problem of the one and the many because it is in seeking a
response to this problem that theories of participation arise:

> Wherever there is a multiplicity of members all of
> which possess some common attribute there must also
> be some one superior source possessing the same
> attribute in unmixed purity and perfection, from
> which each of the inferior recipients derives its own
> diminished and imperfect participation.[12]

The relationship of this problem to the notion of participation features powerfully in Plato: "There is an absolute
beauty and an absolute good, and of other things to which
the term 'many' is applied there is an absolute; for they may
be brought under a single idea, which is the essence of

---

[11] Ibid., 84.
[12] Clarke, *Explorations*, 90.

each."[13] Famously, in Plato the exact nature of the participation of the *world of sense* in the *world of ideas* is left vague and obscure; it has been argued that Plato himself explicitly recognized this as a defect of his philosophy.[14] In any case, dissatisfied both with Aristotle's dismissal of any notion of metaphysical participation, and with Platonic ambiguity in this area, Aquinas attempts a full definition of the term:

> To participate is to receive as it were a part; and therefore when anything receives in a particular manner that which belongs to another in a universal [or total] manner, it is said to participate it; as man is said to participate animal, because he does not possess the intelligible notes (*ratio*) of animal according to the latter's total "community" [i.e., universality]; and for the same reason Socrates participates man; in like manner also a subject participates an accident, and matter form, because the substantial or accidental form, which of itself as such is common [or unparticularized], is determined to this or that subject; and similarly an effect is said to participate its cause, and especially when it does not equal the power of its cause, as, for example, if we say that air participates the light of the sun because it does not receive it with the same brightness that it has in the sun.[15]

Here Aquinas not only gives us the fundamental structure of what is entailed by the notion of participation, but also its

---

[13] *Republic*, 507b.

[14] See John F. Wippel, *The Metaphysical Thought of Thomas Aquinas* (Washington: Catholic University of America Press, 2000), 96.

[15] Thomas Aquinas, *In Boeth. de Hebdom.* lect. 2, in *An Exposition of the On the Hebdomads of Boethius,* trans. Janice L. Schultz and Edward A. Synan (Washington: Catholic University of America Press, 2001).

highly analogical character. This is the single most complete analysis in Aquinas's writings, but one finds the following three briefer quasi-definitions in other places which do not substantially differ from the more extensive account above:

> To participate is nothing else than to receive partially from another.[16]

> A subject is finite with reference to that which it participates, because that which is participated is received in the participant not according to its total infinity but in a particular manner.[17]

> Whatever is participated is determined to the mode of that which is participated and is thus possessed in a partial way and not according to every mode of perfection.[18]

These quotations can be explained in the following way: *esse* is determined by the participant subject (essence), and in being so determined is not possessed in its fullness, but rather is limited to the existence of *this* or *that* finite being. No single participant subject, nor all participant subjects together, can exhaust *esse*. For this reason we have called *esse* an "all-encompassing plenitude."

For Aquinas, then, there are three essential components to any participation structure. First, there must be a source which possesses the perfection in question in a total and unrestricted manner. Secondly, there must be a participating subject possessing the perfection in question in a partial or

---

[16] *In De Caelo et Mundo*, 12, 18, 8.

[17] *Super Librum de causis Expositio*, lect. 4, XXI, 725A.

[18] Thomas Aquinas, *Summa Contra Gentiles*, I, 32, trans. Anton C. Pegis (Indiana: University of Notre Dame Press, 1976).

restricted manner. And thirdly, since this participating sub-ject is a negative principle, having no prior existence of its own, it must receive the perfection in question *from*, or due to dependence on, the higher source.

Aquinas articulates this when he says that "whatever pos-sesses something by participation is traced back (or drawn back: *reducitur*) to that which possesses it by essence, as to its principle and cause."[19] Whatever, then, has the three compo-nents listed above is some kind of participation structure; this means that the term can be applied differently according to that to which it refers:

> The totality and dependence involved may be either in the purely logical order of subordination of concepts by extension, or in the purely formal order of similarity and dependence resulting from exemplarity, or imply-ing even efficient causality whenever the participation touches the order of existence as such.[20]

The very term "participation," therefore, is merely a tech-nical way of expressing the complex of relations involved in any structure of dependence of some lower multiplicity on a higher source for similarity of nature. Aquinas thus uses the term for expressing the radical dependence of all contingent beings on God both for their origin and their analogical imita-

---

[19] Thomas Aquinas, *Compendium of Theology*, trans. Richard J. Regan (New York: Oxford University Press, 2009), c. 68, II, 37. See also *Summa Con. Gen.*, III, 69; *Quaestiones Disputatae De Potentia Dei*, trans. English Dominican Fathers (Westminster, MD: The Newman Press, 1952), q. 6, art. 6; *Disputed Questions on Spiritual Creatures*, trans. Mary C. Fitzpatrick and John J. Wellmuth (Milwaukee: Marquette University Press, 1949), art. 10; *Commentary on Aristotle's Metaphysics*, trans. John P. Rowan (n.p.: Dumb Ox Books, 1995), lect. 2.

[20] Clarke, *Explorations*, 93.

tion of his very essence. This only works, of course, if Aquinas can provide a basic perfection shared by both God and creatures, which must be the core of all perfections possessed by them. This is exactly what is satisfied by Thomas's doctrine of *esse*, the act of existence. The precise nature of God's imitability, and how finite beings achieve this imitation by participation, is the topic of the first section of the next chapter.

Aquinas's entire ontology is a single participation structure, within which are substructures of participation accounting for the various relations within the matrix of contingent reality. In this ontology, whatever is the source must be by definition that which is the "ultimate font of the perfection in question."[21] The source cannot receive the perfection from something else; it must possess it by virtue of its own essence. The essence of the source must be identical and convertible with this perfection; if it were merely to *have* the perfection as part of its essence, it too would be a participant.[22] In turn, it cannot merely *have* the perfection, it must *be* this perfection, and *be* it in purity and simplicity.

Aquinas posits in the following way the difference between the essential possession of a perfection and the possession of a perfection by participation:

[21] Ibid., 94.

[22] "Convertible" is used here in the technical scholastic sense, i.e., two or more principles differing not in reality but in aspect only. For example, Aquinas holds that truth, goodness, unity, and beauty are "transcendental attributes of being," i.e., can be attributed to all that *is*, and are not simply attributes of certain instances of being, like *green*, *big*, or *fast*. In turn, the transcendental attributes are identical and convertible with being; they denote being under different aspects. In finite beings essence and *esse* are really distinct, but in God are distinct only in aspect, for they are identical to, and convertible with, one another.

46

> Something is predicated of a subject in two ways:
> in one way by essence, in the other by participation;
> for light is predicated of an illuminated body by partici-
> pation, but if there existed some separated [i.e., pure
> or unmixed] light it would be predicated of it by
> essence.[23]

And again,

> That which is totally something does not participate it
> but is by essence identified with it. What, however, is
> not totally identified with something but has something
> else joined with it is properly said to participate.[24]

Two important notions follow from the source possessing
a perfection by essence, and so without composition. First,
the source must be unique, for were there two sources both
possessing the same perfection by essence in perfect simplicity, they could not be in any way distinguished. Second, the
perfection must be infinite in the source. The reason for this
is the same as that for its unicity: the perfection is present in
perfect simplicity, therefore it forms no "mixture" with
something else which could limit it. As we have said,
Aquinas's entire ontology is a single participation structure,
and the source on which this structure depends must be,
then, perfectly simple, unique, and infinite.

It should now be evident that it is deeply misleading to
suggest that the worldview of Aquinas is simply one of a
"baptized Aristotelianism." Furthermore, what has been
advanced should already indicate that the Five Ways do not
represent Aquinas's own path to God via unaided reason,

---

[23] *Quodlibet* II, 2, 3.
[24] *In I Met.* lect. 10, no. 154.

Ways which I will submit are presented for quite another purpose (to be analyzed in depth in Section 2 of Chapter 3).

Having considered for a moment the source of the participation structure, let us turn to consider the participant subject. It cannot be *simple*, for it does not possess its perfection as its essence, but rather is composed of both the perfection received and the subject which receives it:

> Whenever anything is predicated of another by participation, it is necessary that there be present there something other than what is participated; and therefore in every creature which has existence the creature itself which has *esse* is "other" than the *esse* which it has.[25]

Every participant subject is a composition, and is limited, and is therefore distinguished from its source. This is what gives us the key to the radical metaphysical structure of all finite beings in Aquinas's ontology, whether in the order of essence-existence or that of matter-form. These two orders of principles respond to different problems regarding finite beings. The order of essence and existence responds to the question of limitation and infinity in giving an account of the identity and being of a thing. The order of matter and form seeks to give an account of the intrinsic structure of the physical or sensible things of our experience, the existence of which is accounted for by the former principles.

What we have been describing is little more than a "reworking of the basic framework of participation as handed down to St. Thomas by the Neoplatonic tradition."[26] What is unique in the history of participation metaphysics is the

---

[25] *Quodlibet* II, 2, 3.
[26] Clarke, *Explorations*, 95.

transposition executed by Aquinas of its entire structure "into the technical Aristotelian framework of metaphysical composition in terms of act and potency."[27] This transposition is articulated clearly in the following passage:

> Every subject which participates something is compared to that which it participates as potency to act: for by that which it participates it becomes in act such a participant. . . . Therefore every created substance is compared to its act of existence as potency to act.[28]

Aquinas recognized that the problem with the Neoplatonic ontology to which he was heir was the lack of metaphysical explanation for the intrinsic unity of the compositions resulting in finite beings from participation. In turn, he transposed this ontology into the only adequate theory of unity in metaphysical composition so far developed, i.e., "the Aristotelian doctrine of act and potency as correlative, incomplete metaphysical principles, intrinsically ordered one to the other so as to form a *per se* unit."[29] This transposition is an explicit move made by Aquinas: "In every composite there must be act and potency. For a plurality cannot become simply one unless there be there something which is act and something else which is potency."[30]

In this metaphysical schema act and potency are "de-Aristotelianized," so to speak, no longer referring merely to change and motion. Potency had always entailed some ordering toward a future actuation, like, for example, that of an

---

[27] Ibid., 95.
[28] *Summa Con. Gen.* II, 53.
[29] Clarke, *Explorations*, 96.
[30] *Summa Con. Gen.* I, 18.

acorn being ordered toward the actuation of an oak; but Aquinas adapts potency to a new static role as limiting, receiving subject. Out of this comes the widely known Thomistic principle: *Pure or unreceived act is infinite; act is limited only by reception in a really distinct potency.*[31] What we are uncovering here is a truly original synthesis:

> It is impossible to understand this . . . in terms either of pure Aristotelianism or pure Neoplatonism. It is not pure Aristotelianism, because Aristotle (like Plato), accepted the classical Greek notion of the finite as the perfect and the infinite as the imperfect; hence there is not only no mention but no place in his system for a theory of act as infinite and potency as limit. Nor is it pure Neoplatonism, because no Neoplatonist had ever used Aristotelian act and potency to express participation. This synthesis is peculiarly the work of St. Thomas's own genius, fusing into an organic unity the best of these two main streams of Western philosophy.[32]

As mentioned earlier, there are two sets of principles to which participation is especially pertinent, namely *matter-form* and *essence-existence*. It is the latter principles which are of primary metaphysical value, for it is by these that we ascend to the source, that is, to God. This is because the only example where "the source of a participated perfection enjoys genuine ontological subsistence as a positive, intensive plenitude is in the case of the transcendental analogous perfections, all reducible to *esse*, whose source is God, *Ipsum Esse*

---

[31] *Summa Con. Gen.* I, 43: "An act existing in nothing is limited (*terminatur*) by nothing"; *Compend. Theologiae*, c. 18: "No act is found to be limited except through a potency which is a receptive power (*vis receptiva*)."

[32] Clarke, *Explorations*, 96.

Subsistens.[33] No finite being can be said to be perfectly subsistent in this way, for it possesses being, as well as goodness, unity, and any other transcendental perfection, only by participation, and not by essence.

For Aquinas, *the one,* as the source of *the many,* may be merely analogous in similarity, and not necessarily univocal. That is, for example, when "goodness" is predicated of both God and a tree, this attribute is not predicated *metaphorically* in either case, but *is* predicated *equivocally,* for although both the tree and God are *literally* "good," there is an *infinite* difference between what is meant by the goodness of God and that of a tree. In turn, he "sweeps away with a single stroke the vast Neoplatonic superstructure of subsistent specific, generic, and accidental forms, reducing them all to dependence on a single ontological source in the order of the one basic ontological perfection of *esse.*"[34] Aquinas therefore concludes that this source can be nothing other than God Himself, the efficient cause of all being, rendering the world intelligible in its multiplicity as the ultimate exemplary cause of every form by the ideas of the divine mind, the Eternal Logos.

Reconciling different interpretations of Aquinas's participation metaphysics

I have alluded to those who comprise what may be termed the "first wave" of Thomistic "participationists," i.e., Fabro and Geiger, the scholars who initiated the recovery of Aquinas's Neoplatonism in the mid-twentieth century. So far I have relied heavily upon the scholarship of Clarke, on the

[33] Ibid., 97.
[34] Ibid.

grounds that he came a little later and could therefore draw on the insights of Fabro and Geiger with the benefit of distance. Beyond this, Clarke also tested the veracity of their claims by extensive comparisons with the primary sources, and due to both his rigor and lucidity his work is widely trusted. My own particular application of Clarke so far has merely been to achieve an historical sketch of thought regarding metaphysical participation, and to construct a clear idea of what such participation *per se* entails. Now, however, it is necessary to look more closely at the work of Fabro and Geiger, at their own writings and approaches, as well as their disagreements. By doing this many of the more subtle distinctions which have hitherto remained implicit will be brought to the foreground. Despite their close interests, these two men never reached full agreement. But more recently Wippel has argued that their interpretations of Thomistic participation were incompatible only in appearance, and in turn has sought to reconcile their respective positions. We shall, then, conclude this chapter with an assessment of Wippel's reception of the works of Fabro and Geiger.[35]

Fabro claims that he identifies in Aquinas's ontology two fundamental modes of participation, namely what he terms "predicamental-univocal participation" and "transcendental-analogical participation." In the first mode we discover that all independent participant subjects which share a common formality do so through their essential content. These indi-

---

[35] Much of Fabro and Geiger remains only in Italian and French respectively, and so I will be relying on the few works now in English, and the translations made of the pieces deemed more important by Wippel and his student, Gregory T. Doolan, as well as—in the case of Fabro —my own translations.

vidual substances participate in a shared existence received by all, but this shared existence is not itself anything independently of such participant subjects.[36] In turn, predicamental participation refers to *real* participation when applied to matter participating in a form or a subject in its accidents, and to purely *logical* participation (for example, that of a sportsman in a game) when there is question of the existence of things.

In contrast to this first mode, transcendental participation refers specifically to the possession by finite beings of the transcendental attributes; that is, the participation of participant subjects in some perfection "according to a deficiency of likeness."[37] The perfection in question here has an existence of its own independently of the participant, "either as a property of a higher entity or in itself as a pure and subsistent formality in its full possession, for example, as beings (*entia*) participate in *esse*."[38] The participated perfection is shared in by participant subjects according to different degrees, and therefore cannot be predicated of them univocally. Transcendental participation is, then, an analogical mode, and Fabro considers it to be the primary meaning of the term "participation" for Aquinas.[39]

Fabro, in turn, regards any finite substance to be something whose existence involves two kinds of participation: it participates in a *real* way according to the transcendental order in that it is a composite of essence and *esse*, and it participates in a *real* way according to the predicamental order in

---

[36] See Cornelio Fabro, C.P.S., *La nozione metafisica di partecipazione* 2nd ed. (Turin: Società Editrice Internazionale, 1963), 317–18.

[37] Gregory T. Doolan, *Aquinas on the Divine Ideas as Exemplar Causes* (Washington, DC: Catholic University of America Press, 2008), 200.

[38] Ibid.

[39] See Fabro, *La nozione*, 318.

that it is a composite of matter and form, or of substance and accidents.[40] Fabro sees these two orders to be closely related, for together they convey the complete structure of a finite substance from the perspective of participation. Clearly he places greater importance on the composition of essence and *esse* within a single substance, for he thinks—as I have argued Aquinas does too—that it is by this that the human mind may ascend to God:

> Since the essence of a creature has also its own partici-
> pated act of being (*actus essendi*), its actualization is not
> merely a relation of extrinsic dependence; rather, it is
> based on the act of *esse* in which it participates and
> which it preserves within itself and is the proper termi-
> nus of divine causality.[41]

Like Fabro, Geiger also identifies two modes of participation in Aquinas's ontology, which he names "participation by composition" and "participation by similitude" (the latter he also refers to as "formal hierarchy"). The first kind of participation makes reference to the fact that, in order for participation to occur, there must be a receiver and something received. It is this that gives an account of metaphysical limitation, which in turn accounts for the fundamental structure of finite beings—for example, the reception (and therefore *limitation*) by a participant subject of *esse* (or indeed the other transcendental attributes convertible with *esse*), or the reception of form by matter. Since that which receives is less perfect than the perfection received, the former limits the latter.

---

[40] Cornelio Fabro, C.P.S. "The Intensive Hermeneutics of Thomistic Philosophy: The Notion of Participation," *Review of Metaphysics* 27.3 (1974): 449–91; 480–81.

[41] Ibid., 481.

Geiger makes clear his meaning of "participation by composition": "The *reception* and consequently the *possession* of an element playing the role of form by a subject playing the role of matter."[42] For example, the form "dog" can be accommodated by many configurations of matter, so long as the matter can possess those parts essential to dogs. Nevertheless there is an existent being of this kind only when the form "dog" is limited to the matter of *this* greyhound, or *that* pug. So too, many things *can* exist, but existence is only a component of something *real* when it is limited by *this* or *that* essence.

Participation by similitude, on the other hand, "expresses the diminished, particularized, and, in this sense, participated state of an essence each time it is not realized in the absolute fullness of its formal content."[43] To return to our last example, both the greyhound and the pug (or any instance of any other breed) imitate the form "dog" for their perfection, but neither realizes the fullness of the formal content of "dog." In turn, if two or more beings both imitate the same source for their perfection, they do so to their own particular degrees.

Geiger distinguishes these two modes of participation by how they respectively explain the notion of limitation. Participation by composition aims at explaining the limitation by a participant subject of a received perfection, relating to each other as potency to act. On the other hand, participation by similitude seeks to account for the "receiver" itself, i.e., explain the participant subject, or *negative principle*, which is

---

[42] Louis-Bertrand Geiger, O.P., *La participation dans la philosophie de s. Thomas d'Aquin*, 2nd ed. (Paris: Librairie Philosophique J. Vrin, 1953), 27–28.

[43] Ibid., 28–29.

metaphysically prior to any reception of, and composition with, its proper perfection.

These two modes of participation, according to Geiger, belong to two different philosophical traditions and two different periods in history: participation by composition belonging to classical Platonism, whereas participation by similitude belongs to later Neoplatonism.[44] He claims that both modes are traceable in Aquinas. Geiger argues that in fact they refer to quite separate problems, with participation by composition offering an account of the complex structures of the beings of our experience, which gives rise to the problem of what accounts for the essences of such beings. This question of the origin of essences finds its response in the theory of participation by similitude. Geiger holds, then, that Aquinas's participation metaphysics is not only a synthesis of the Neoplatonic and Aristotelian ontologies, but also a synthesis of two distinct notions of participation belonging to two different Platonic traditions, uniting them as complementary currents in a more comprehensive ontology.[45] The complementarity of these two modes can be grasped by the fact that participation by composition cannot explain the origin of either formal multiplicity or the participant subjects which limit forms, and participation by similitude cannot explain the composition of form and matter, subject and its accidents, or essence and *esse*. According to Geiger, Aquinas saw that neither mode was sufficient without the other.[46]

As stated, the mode of participation which refers to matter in form, and subject in its accidents, involves composi-

[44] See Doolan, *Aquinas on the Divine Ideas*, 201–2.

[45] Geiger, *La participation*, 29–30.

[46] Ibid., 392–98.

tion. This composition accounts for limitation in regard to the principles just mentioned, but according to Geiger there must be a prior limitation to account for the subject of the composition. He also points out that the notion of participation which refers to that of an effect in its cause also implies some prior limitation; for an effect is produced by its cause, but an "effect cannot receive before it even exists the very thing that makes it to be—in short, its limitation must precede its composition."[47]

Like any Thomist, Geiger holds that a contingent being is composed of two really distinct principles, essence and *esse*, with the former as the principle of limitation. However, he questions how *esse* can be limited by a purely "negative principle," that is, it seems incoherent to assign a function to a principle which does not exist. He posits that essence can be accounted for independently by reference to a kind of participation prior to that of composition, namely that of formal hierarchy "by which participants share in a greater or lesser likeness to the First Perfection."[48] Geiger describes this in the following way: "The essence that participates *in* existence is itself a participation *of* the First Perfection, of which it conveys only a limited and fragmentary aspect."[49] The principle of essence, then, is a created emanation of the divine essence, to which *esse* is granted, conveying a "limited and fragmentary aspect" of its source.

Both Fabro and Geiger interpret Aquinas in such a way as to draw out a twofold theory of participation, and the respective divisions made by them share some similarity, as

---

[47] Doolan, *Aquinas on the Divine Ideas*, 203.

[48] Ibid.

[49] Geiger, *La participation*, 60–61.

would be expected. There are, however, profound differences. Geiger gives primacy to participation by similitude to account for the limitation of *esse* in finite beings; in contrast Fabro gives primacy to transcendental-analogical participation. Fundamentally, Fabro concludes that Geiger departs from Aquinas's view of the relationship between essence and *esse* in finite beings by making too strict a division between participation by composition and participation by similitude. The divisions of Fabro and Geiger can be presented in the following way:

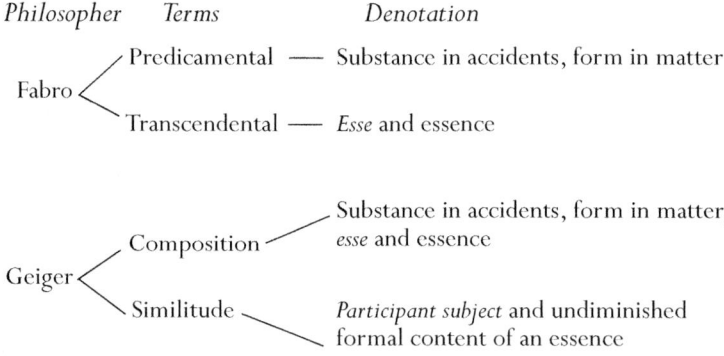

Philosopher   *Terms*   *Denotation*

Fabro
- Predicamental —— Substance in accidents, form in matter
- Transcendental —— *Esse* and essence

Geiger
- Composition —— Substance in accidents, form in matter, *esse* and essence
- Similitude —— *Participant subject* and undiminished formal content of an essence

Until recently it has generally been judged by those with an interest in participation metaphysics that the views of Fabro and Geiger are irreconcilable, and scholars have tended to side with one or the other in interpreting Aquinas. Wippel, however, has sought to integrate the two interpretations into a single approach. In his magnum opus, *The Metaphysical Thought of Thomas Aquinas*, Wippel argues that many of the disagreements regarding the proper interpretation of Aquinas's participation metaphysics stem from a lack of sensitivity toward the different ways Thomas uses the term "*esse*." Sometimes he is referring to *esse commune* (defined below), sometimes to *esse subsistens* (i.e., God), and at other times to the individual *actus essendi* of contingent beings. Wippel argues that *esse*—when we are not speaking of God's *Esse*—is always a kind of participation which corresponds to that of an effect in its cause, especially when the effect is not equal in power to that cause.

Participation in *esse commune* refers to the notion that every finite being shares in *esse* without possessing it essentially. Participation in *esse commune* simply means that finite contingent beings are precisely finite and contingent, for they are not identical with *esse*. This does not mean however that *esse commune* exists independently of these beings (apart from as an abstraction in the mind); just as Socrates really participates whiteness, even though whiteness does not exist apart from him and others with the same attribute.

In Wippel's view, often when Aquinas speaks of participation in *esse* he is referring to participation in *esse subsistens*, or the "First Act," or "First *Esse*." Generally Aquinas adds that such participation is by some "likeness," or imitation. By such a qualification Aquinas is being clear that he ought not to be read as a pantheist; he is not positing that created beings possess some small part of God's *esse*. Rather, each finite being has a particular likeness to the divine *esse*, for each possesses its own *actus essendi*, which has God as its efficient cause. The divine nature itself remains uncommunicated and unparticipated; nevertheless its *likeness* is communicated to all created beings.[50] Both the *actus essendi* of each finite being, and the *esse commune* of all finite being, depend upon *esse subsistens*—the First *Esse*—for their explanation, which is the exemplar,

---

[50] Wippel, *The Metaphysical Thought*, 120–21.

efficient, and final cause of every created substance.[51] Finite beings participate in *esse commune* for they merely *have esse*, they are not themselves *esse*; they have their own *actus essendi*, for they are not one but many. Moreover, Wippel argues that participation in *esse commune* does not supplant participation in *esse subsistens*, since, as we have said, the metaphysical foundation for the former is the latter; it is due to the likeness of finite beings to *esse subsistens* that they participate in *esse commune*.[52]

Having made these distinctions between the different uses of "*esse*" in Aquinas, Wippel turns to assess the debate between Fabro and Geiger in order to judge whether their respective approaches are truly irreconcilable. First, Wippel points out that Fabro's division of transcendental and predicamental participation, and Geiger's division of participation by composition and by similitude, are interpretations; neither sets of terms appears as such in Aquinas. These terms are simply an attempt to make sense of, and systematize, Aquinas's participation metaphysics as it is found in a scattered fashion throughout his works.[53]

Wippel deems Geiger's terminology preferable, but alters it somewhat. In all cases of real (not merely logical) participation, the participant and participated perfection are united as potency to act. Like Clarke, Wippel holds that this accounts for the relation in a finite being between essence and the being's own *actus essendi*. As *act* is not *per se* self-limiting; limited *esse* in finite beings must be accounted for by reference to the notion of *act* being received and limited by a really distinct

---

[51] Ibid., 116.
[52] Ibid., 120–21.
[53] Ibid., 95.

principle of potency. Wippel concludes then that limitation is accounted for by the composition of the really distinct principles of essence and *esse*. In turn, while opting for the terminology of Geiger, Wippel follows Fabro in setting apart the composition of *esse* and essence as more fundamental than any other kind of metaphysical composition.[54]

Geiger holds that the notion of participation by composition relies upon that of participation by similitude, otherwise one would be led to a view of pre-existing essences whose existence cannot be explained (for by definition they cannot possess any *act of existence*). Wippel contests this conclusion, showing that Aquinas clearly judges the essence of a finite being to be created simultaneously with its *actus essendi*. Geiger, due to what Wippel considers his overly severe divisions of participation, fails to acknowledge that causes can simultaneously be causes of one another, and hence principles can be mutually dependent upon one another. What is prior in the order of time is not necessarily so in the metaphysical order. For example, the act of existence (*esse*) causes a finite being to exist by actualizing its essence; it is equally true however that the essence simultaneously receives and limits that *esse* principle (causing it in turn to be that essence's own *actus essendi*). Neither principle exists apart from the other, and each is metaphysically prior in regard to its ontological function.[55]

Having criticized Geiger, and argued for the truth of Fabro's position regarding the role of composition in Aquinas's participation metaphysics, Wippel then argues in defense of what he deems true in Geiger's interpretation.[56]

---

[54] Ibid., 128.
[55] Ibid., 129–30.
[56] See ibid., 130.

Whilst agreeing with Fabro's emphasis on composition to account for the *existent* and *essential* structure of finite beings as the most fundamental level of their metaphysical constitution, Wippel agrees with Geiger that the essence principle is not fully accounted for by this alone. Paramount for my purposes is the reasoning entailed by Geiger's "participation by similitude," for by it we arrive at a theory of the divine ideas, which is the core topic of Chapter 3.

Doolan notes that Geiger moves in a more metaphysically Platonic direction in holding that "participation by composition must ultimately entail causal dependence in the orders of both efficient and exemplar causality inasmuch as God wills a created being to imitate his divine essence according to its proper respect."[57] The origin of created essences can be accounted for only by a theory of participation by similitude (formal hierarchy).[58]

Wippel judges that both Fabro and Geiger seized something true in their interpretations, and both are necessary for a full understanding of Aquinas's participation metaphysics. It is worth noting, however, that participation by composition is first in the *order of discovery* for the philosopher. "Looking at finite beings, the philosopher is able to discern that they must participate in *esse commune* and that this participation entails a real distinction within them between the essence principle and the *actus essendi*."[59] Participation of finite beings in *esse subsistens* can be discerned inasmuch as God is judged to be efficient, exemplar, and final cause of all contingent reality.

57 Doolan, *Aquinas on the Divine Ideas*, 210.
58 Wippel, *The Metaphysical Thought*, 130.
59 Doolan, *Aquinas on the Divine Ideas*, 210.

This, however, presupposes that God's existence has already been demonstrated, which is last in the order of discovery for the philosopher, for it is the demonstration furthest from experience. Hence, participation by similitude, or formal hierarchy, follows participation by composition in the order of philosophical discovery. Nevertheless, participation by similitude takes priority over composition according to the *order of metaphysics*, which gives priority to the *why* over the *what* of things. Wippel explains:

> Creatures actually exist because God wills them to exist and efficiently causes them. But God can will a creature of a certain kind to exist only if it can exist. And it can exist only if it is viewed by God as a possible way of imitating the divine essence.[60]

As we have argued at length, any metaphysical participation structure involves the reception in a particular way of a perfection that another possesses in a universal way. Thus, a participant subject possesses a participated perfection in a limited way, not according to its fullness. The purpose, then, of participation metaphysics is simply to explain how a single perfection can be possessed by many different finite beings, i.e., its purpose is to answer the ancient problem of the one and the many. Beyond the participant and participated perfection there is a third element, namely that "everything that participates something receives it from that *from which* it participates, and in this respect that from which it participates is its cause."[61] Moreover, as stated, the participant subject

---

[60] Wippel, *The Metaphysical Thought*, 131.

[61] Aquinas, *De sub. sep.*, c. 3.

stands as potency to that which is received, which stands as act.[62] Here is Aquinas's own clear explanation:

> Everything that is after the First Being, since it is not its *esse*, has an *esse* that is received in something through which that *esse* is contracted. Thus in every creature the nature of the thing that participates *esse* is other than that participated *esse*. And since every thing participates in the First Act through assimilation inasmuch as it has *esse*, the participated *esse* in each thing must be compared to the nature that participates in it as act to potency.[63]

We have, then, a twofold participation: essence participates in *esse*, limiting *esse* as potency to act; this received *act* is the participant subject's own individual *actus essendi*. Beyond this however the participant subject participates in the First Act—the First Being—by way of assimilation, receiving in a limited way a likeness of the divine essence.[64]

Holding these approaches together we see that the divine essence remains itself unparticipated (i.e., utterly transcendent, thus avoiding pantheism); it is not understood to enter into any composition with finite beings. Rather, it is the *likeness* of the divine essence which is participated.[65] A created essence, then, is a *likeness* of the uncreated essence in which it has its exemplar, and in receiving *esse* the finite being is a likeness of the one whose essence is existence. This first *likeness* is

---

[62] *Summa Theo.* I, 75, 5 ad 1.

[63] *De Spir. Creat.* art. 1.

[64] See Aquinas, *Commentary on the Sentences*, I, 36, 2, 2; *Summa Theo.* I, 15, 2; *Summa Theo.* I, 44, 3.

[65] Aquinas, *In librum B. Dionysii De divinis nominibus expositio*, ch. 2, lect. 3, no. 158. https://aquinas.cc

the principle of all principles which enter into composition with the received perfection of *esse*; in turn, participation by composition ultimately depends upon participation by similitude. This is indeed Wippel's conclusion: Aquinas's participation metaphysics entails composition *and* assimilation.[66]

There is a *real* (ontological) distinction between the divine idea and the creature of which it is the exemplar; there is no composition between the former and the latter. If there were such a composition, "God's essence would enter into the composition of a creature since the divine ideas are ontologically the same as the divine essence."[67] If the divine ideas were not identical to the divine essence, God would Himself be a composition of parts, and therefore would need an explanation beyond Himself, and so would not be God. Although, then, there is this *real* distinction, assimilation also "involves a real relation of finite being (*ens*) to its divine idea since a finite being is really dependent upon its exemplar idea in order for it to exist as that being."[68] Via Geiger's "participation by similitude" united to Fabro's realism, we have moved from participation as only a means by which to explain the metaphysical structure of finite substances to participation as a way of "looking into" the divine mind, the Eternal Logos, by grasping the world as a picture of it.

We have now arrived at the point at which we can further draw out, from a theory of participation, a theory of *divine exemplarism*. In doing so, Doolan points out that there are new questions which require answers: What is it exactly that stands in likeness to the divine idea? Is it only the essence of

---

[66] Wippel, *The Metaphysical Thought*, 118, 131.
[67] Doolan, *Aquinas on the Divine Ideas*, 213.
[68] Ibid.

the finite being, or that being's entirety, as an *essentia-esse* composition?[69] It is the relation of the world of finite beings to the mind of God which will be the first topic of the next chapter.

[69] Ibid., 228.

3

Participation Metaphysics and Divine Exemplarism

God is the infinite perfection of every sort.
—Giovanni Pico della Mirandola,
On Being and the One

The world and the divine mind

WE HAVE OBSERVED that in Plato the nature of the relationship of the world to the unchanging and perfect forms is left ambiguous. We have already gone some way to explaining the relationship of the world to the ideas as exemplar causes in the divine mind; nevertheless we must leave no stone unturned, so to speak. This chapter will attempt to complete the picture, so that a fuller account of Aquinas's Neoplatonic ontology may be presented.

In the disputed questions *De Veritate* Aquinas appears to advance the view that a thing's being (*esse*) is a component of the divine idea of that thing.[1] He states the following:

> Although . . . a natural agent is only the cause of coming-to-be (*fiendi*)—a sign of which is that upon its destruction the being (*esse*) of the thing [effect] does

[1] Thomas Aquinas, *Questiones Disputatae de Veritate*, q. 2, a. 3, ad 20, trans. Robert W. Mulligan, S.J. (Chicago: Henry Regnery Company, 1952).

not cease but only [its] coming-to-be (*fieri*)—the divine agent that is imparting (*influens*) being (*esse*) to things is still the cause of the act of being (*esse*) for all things, even though he does not enter into the constitution of things; and he is still the likeness of the essential principles that enter into the constitution of a thing. Therefore he knows not only the coming-to-be of a thing but its act of being and its essential principles.

Although Aquinas does not here explicitly refer to the divine ideas by name, he is nevertheless discussing exemplar causation in the context of divine knowledge. According to this passage, it seems that God's knowledge of a thing includes its essential principles *and* its act of being (*esse*). As God knows the world through the divine ideas, we can infer that "a divine idea is the exemplar of both the essence and *esse* principles of a finite being."[2]

Doolan argues, on the contrary, that Aquinas should be read in such a way as to mean that it is a finite being's essence alone which corresponds to the divine idea, and not its entirety as an essence-*esse* composition. The essence of a thing is the likeness of its exemplar idea in the divine mind; it is because God imparts being to a thing that he knows the thing's act of existence, not because he has an idea of it.

The argument runs as follows. God knows the essence of a thing via his idea of it; on the other hand to know the existence of a thing is not to know *what* it is, but only to know *that* it is, and God knows *that* something is for he is the ultimate efficient cause of its existence. Since God is such a cause, and "knowledge is only productive through the mediation of the

---

[2] Doolan, *Aquinas on the Divine Ideas*, 215.

will," it is the divine will which unifies the different modes of divine knowledge in the creative act, granting existence to a created essence which has the potential to exist.[3] God, then, knows the *being* of a thing as its efficient cause, and the *essence* of a thing as its exemplar cause. In this way the two modes of God's knowledge address both efficient and formal causality. In turn, God knows the entirety of a finite being via the unifying and mediating divine will in his single creative act.

To use the terminology of Geiger, the specific relation of created essences to their divine exemplars is that of participation by similitude. Fabro too, at one point, appears to present this view:

> To the extent that participation allows one to conceive the created universe in the complexity of its natures as a reflection of divine ideas or exemplars, one may speak of participation by similitude (*per similitudinem*) in the transcendental order according to a relation of dependence of the finite on the Infinite.[4]

The divine ideas "act as intermediaries through which created essences are derived from divine essence."[5] We find a reverse image of this notion in human epistemology, with ideas in the human mind being intermediary abstractions from experience of external beings, by which the intelligence seizes the intelligibility of the world, not so that the one whose intelligence it is may know these ideas, but rather that he may know the world of which these ideas are abstractions.

For Aquinas, the essence principle of a finite being is something akin to an *imitation* of an idea in God's mind. This

[3] Ibid., 216.
[4] Fabro, "The Intensive Hermeneutics," 476.
[5] Doolan, *Aquinas on the Divine Ideas*, 218.

is what is expressed by Geiger's view that the finite nature of created essence must depend upon a prior participation by similitude.[6]

We can speak, then, of a twofold divine exemplarism: that of the divine ideas, and that of the divine nature. The latter involves the divine attributes, such as goodness and truth and beauty (which Aquinas holds can be predicated of God without reference to *revealed religion*). Creatures can be compared to God analogically in different ways according to his attributes; thus "Thomas describes a twofold likeness between creatures and God: in one way, creatures are like the divine ideas, but in another way, they are like the divine nature."[7]

An Aristotelian argument for God's existence can be found in any one of the Five Ways, tracing back to an *Uncaused First Cause* from the existence of finite contingent beings. A more Platonic way of mentally ascending to God begins not only with the existence of things, but with the essences of things. In Aquinas's twofold exemplarism we reach God by a synthesis of these approaches, enabling us not only to say *that* God is, but something of *what* he is.

In the following extended quotation, Doolan shows how the Thomist approach presents the world as a *picture* of God, and in so doing draws on an example favored by Aquinas, namely that of the artist:

> If we consider the foundation of exemplarism and real participation, I suggest that we find the following logical "moments": in the first moment, there is the divine essence, or nature, which is imitable in itself; in the

---

[6] See Wippel, *The Metaphysical Thought*, 130.
[7] Doolan, *Aquinas on the Divine Ideas*, 219.

second moment, God knows his nature as imitable and thus "discovers" ideas; in the third moment, he looks to these ideas and, by an act of his will, creates essences in their likeness, simultaneously creating the corresponding acts of being that these essences receive inasmuch as created beings (*entia*) participate in a likeness of the divine nature. Thus, created beings simultaneously share a likeness to both their respective exemplar ideas and to the divine nature. Developing Thomas's analogy from art, we could compare these moments to those of an artist's painting a self-portrait. In the first moment, the artist's likeness is imitable in itself; in the second moment, he has an idea of its imitability; in the third, he paints his likeness, a likeness that is simultaneously similar to both his idea and, in a certain respect, himself as a whole.[8]

The analogy of the artist has its obvious limitations. For the human artist these "moments" are chronologically sequential. God, being beyond time, and there being no *real* distinction between his knowing and willing, knows the world and wills its existence in one simple timeless act. Another fundamental difference between human art and divine exemplarism concerns the radical dependence of the effect on its exemplar, as Aquinas explains:

> An exemplar form is twofold. In one [way it is *that*] *in representation of which* something is made, and for this the form is not required except as a likeness alone— just as we say that real things are the exemplar forms of pictures. In another way an exemplar form is called [*that*] *in likeness of which* something is made and by par-

---

[8] Ibid., 223.

ticipation in which it has an act of being (*esse*), as the divine goodness is the exemplar form of every goodness, and divine wisdom of every wisdom.[9]

Once a painter produces a self-portrait, the painting is not dependent on the artist for its continued existence, and can exist after the artist dies. On the other hand, exemplarism of the divine nature entails the dependence of finite beings for their existence at any given moment on God knowing and willing them to be. For this reason the example of the artist painting a self-portrait is more suitable for explaining the exemplarism of divine ideas. For an analogy of the exemplarism of the divine nature I would opt for that of a musician playing an instrument. Here the music is dependent on it being willed and produced by the musician at every moment; were he to stop playing, the music too would stop.[10]

Exemplarism of the divine nature, as we have said, concerns the transcendental attributes (goodness, beauty, nobility, truth, unity, etc.), for such attributes are held to be convertible with being itself; in turn, merely by its exist-

[9] *In III Sent.*, 27, 2, 4, ad 1.

[10] This is an image used by J.R.R. Tolkien in his *Ainulindalë* creation account at the beginning of *The Silmarillion*. Tolkien describes how the Ainur, a choir of angels who act as "co-creators," give physical being to the world which has hitherto existed only as an idea in the mind of Eru Ilúvatar, the Supreme Being. The Ainur have intimate knowledge of the ideas in the mind of Ilúvatar, and are described as the "children of Ilúvatar's thought." The specific way they co-create the world is by singing the cosmos into being, channeling the power of Ilúvatar with their music. It is by this angelic music that the essences of the world come forth from Ilúvatar's mind, and to which *he* then grants existence. In turn, a likeness of the ideas in the divine mind receives existence and is held in being by the music of the Ainur. See J.R.R. Tolkien, *The Silmarillion* (Boston: Houghton Mifflin Company, 1977), 15–22.

ence, a finite being participates in the likeness of the divine nature. Neither mode of divine exemplarism is the cause of its effect independently of the cause of the other, for a created essence cannot *come into being* without a corresponding act of being, and a creature's act of being must be limited by its created essence. Put another way, "there must be a finite essence that participates in the likeness of the divine nature in order for an act of being to be received."[11]

I have been careful to write only of the participation of created essence in the "*likeness*" of its divine idea, and never of "direct participation." This obviously serves to keep us from implying pantheism, but this still requires further justification. Finite beings cannot participate directly in the divine ideas for at least three reasons. First, the divine ideas are not *principally* ideas of abstract natures and accidental attributes, but ideas of individuals. As Doolan notes, "the essence of each finite being is exemplified by its own idea: thus, for example, the idea of Socrates is the exemplar of his essence."[12] As demonstrated in Section 1 of Chapter 2, for something to *be* essentially, and for it to *be* by participation, are opposites; in turn, if Socrates were Socrates by participation in his divine idea, Socrates would not essentially be Socrates. In this case we would have to deny altogether what Aristotle termed *primary substance*, which is the most fundamental reality of a being. For this reason, finite beings do not participate in the divine ideas of species or genera; to argue for this would be to confuse purely *logical* with *real* participation:

> It must be recalled that when Thomas describes an individual as participating in its species and a species as par-

[11] Doolan, *Aquinas on the Divine Ideas*, 227–28.
[12] Ibid., 228.

ticipating in its genus, he is referring to a logical participation, not a real one. Furthermore, since the divine ideas of species and genera are speculative and not practical, they are only cognitive principles of God's knowledge, not ontological ones by which he creates—a fact that would rule out any real participation of creatures in such ideas. Thus, if we follow the distinction above, the likeness of a creature to the divine idea of either its species or its genus is due to the fact that such an idea is *that in representation of which something is made* rather than *that in likeness of which something is made.*[13]

The distinction at the end of this quotation is helpful; a finite being is a likeness of the idea of its species in that it is one existent representative of the species, but it is a likeness of its exemplar idea in the divine mind in a more precise sense, its essence being a *perfect likeness* of this idea. To be clear, God has ideas of universal essences, corresponding to species and genera, for he creates many things which share in a single essence, like "human" or "dog." However, in creating these things he must know them—and therefore have an idea of them—as individuals, by which he actually brings them into being. Likewise, a man can have an idea of "woman," and an idea of his wife (by which he knows her); but he does not know his wife as the universal "woman," but as *this particular woman* whom he loves.

The second reason finite beings cannot participate directly in their divine exemplar is that such a participation would be either by composition or by similitude. The first option entails some admixture of finite being and the divine nature,

[13] Ibid., 229, n. 105.

which is impossible; whereas the second option entails that the finite being not be *identical* in likeness with its divine idea.

The notion that the essence of a finite being is created in the likeness of its divine idea can be described as the notion of "similitude," but this should not be confused with what is meant by *"participation by similitude."* As stated, what Geiger means by this—for the term is his—is formal hierarchy, whereby participant subjects share a similarity to some perfection to a lesser or greater extent, none of which subjects is identical to that perfection. In turn, unlike the real participation of a finite being in relation to its exemplar, no participant in a formal hierarchy marks the fullness of the likeness in which it participates: No single dog possesses the fullness of the essence "dog," but is always a particularized, and therefore diminished, instance of this universal essence. On the other hand, "Socrates cannot be more or less similar to the divine idea of Socrates: either he is like it or he is not; either he is Socrates or he is not. In short, he enjoys a perfect likeness to his divine idea."[14] It is the fact that two or more beings share a perfection which takes us to a theory of participation by similitude, but it is here that we discover that the ideas to which this division of participation pertains cannot be those by which an actual being is created, for such a being must be preceded by an idea of which it is a perfect likeness. Therefore, in the order of discovery, we move from the cognitive principles of God's knowledge to the ontological ones by which he creates all that constitutes the world.

Thirdly, nowhere does Aquinas himself argue that finite beings participate directly in their ideas, but rather only speaks in terms of "a likeness":

[14] Ibid., 230.

75

Every single creature has a proper species as it participates in some way [in] a likeness of the divine essence.
Hence, inasmuch as God knows his essence as imitable
thusly by such a creature, he knows it as the proper
notion (*ratio*) and idea of that creature. And similarly
regarding others.[15]

Neither the divine essence nor the divine ideas (which are
only conceptually distinct) are themselves participated, but
rather it is their *likeness* which is participated. As Aquinas
teaches, God "knows his essence perfectly; hence he knows it
according to every mode by which it is knowable. But it can
be known not only as it is in itself, but as it is participable
(*participabilis*) according to some mode of likeness by creatures."[16] Put in another way, the world bears such a resem-
blance to God, conveying in part his own perfect
intelligibility, that the world is, as it were, an icon of God.

Any analogy appears to be found wanting. We have used
the image of the painter with his self-portrait, but this
implies a more deist conception, missing the radical depen-
dency of the world on its ultimate cause at any given
moment. We have also used the image of the musician playing
an instrument, but this too misses the radically incarnational
character of the finite material cosmos as an icon of the infinite immaterial substance. It is also questionable that music
can resemble anything in the musician; and were it to resemble something of the musician, whether it can be said to do
so "being a *likeness*" of anything in the musician. Aquinas, in a

---

[15] *Summa Theo.* 1, 15, 2. For other examples of the same view see
Aquinas, *Summa Theo.*, 1, 44, 3; *In I Sent.*, 36, 2, 2.
[16] *Summa Theo.* 1, 15, 2.

beautiful passage, opts for an image similar to that of the musician in his analogy of the world as a language which communicates the divine goodness; in so doing he presents God as both efficient *and* final cause of the world.

> God, through his providence, orders all things to the divine goodness, as to an end; not, of course, in such a way that something adds to his goodness by means of things that are made, but, rather, that the likeness of his goodness, as much as possible, is impressed on things. However, since every created substance must fall short of the perfection of divine goodness, in order that the likeness of divine goodness might be more perfectly communicated to things, it was necessary for there to be a diversity of things, so that what could not be perfectly represented by one thing might be, in more perfect fashion, represented by a variety of things in different ways. For instance, when a man sees that his mental conception cannot be expressed adequately by one spoken word, he multiplies his words in various ways, to express his mental conception though a variety of means. And the eminence of divine perfection may be observed in this fact, that perfect goodness which is present in God in a unified and simple manner cannot be in creatures except in a diversified manner and through a plurality of things. Now, things are differentiated by their possession of different forms from which they receive their species. And thus, the reason for the diversity of forms in things is derived from this end.[17]

So here we have three analogies: the painter, the musician, and the speaker; and I think one needs to hold all three in

---

[17] *Summa Con. Gen.* III, 69, no. 1.

one's mind to draw close to an adequate understanding of Aquinas's theory of exemplarism. I will seek now to summarize Aquinas's position regarding the relation of the world to the divine mind. The divine ideas are exemplar causes, and as such both created essences and all possible accidental predicates are the similitudes of them. This sharing of a likeness does not however entail that such created essences and accidents participate directly in their respective divine exemplars. Though the artist has an idea of his self-portrait and then paints the portrait, the portrait does not participate directly in his idea, but is a likeness of the idea. Inasmuch as finite beings analogously possess the divine attributes (goodness, being, unity, beauty, nobility, etc.), finite beings participate in a likeness of the exemplar that is the divine nature itself. Through this order of participation, a created essence receives and limits *esse*. This limitation—and this is the main point to be derived from Geiger—is itself dependent upon the "ontologically prior formation of the divine idea that determines the created essence's limited mode of being."[18] In turn, the divine nature is imitable in itself, but finite beings *actually* imitate the divine nature because God wills that his creation be an expression of his own inner life.

A created essence is determined by the idea of it in the divine mind, but its actuality is determined by its composition with *esse* as a real finite being which in turn participates as an individual in a likeness of the divine nature. For such a composition to take place, there must be in the divine mind the idea not only of the created essence, but of the individuated essence as an existing thing; this, however, is via the

---

[18] Doolan, *Aquinas on the Divine Ideas*, 242.

mediation of the divine will, which is only *conceptually* distinct from the divine mind. This view of exemplarism safeguards the radical distinction between creature and Creator, whilst maintaining the former as in part a reflection of the latter. "Socrates is indeed exemplified by the divine idea of Socrates, but he is who he is through his very essence, not through participation."[19]

Essence and *esse* in a creature are correlative principles ultimately "because the two modes of *divine exemplarism* are mutually dependent upon each other."[20] While we can conceptually distinguish between God's divine nature and his ideas—and for Aquinas, the distinction is necessary for understanding the structure of finite substances in how they reflect God—in reality God is absolutely simple and therefore is not a composition of parts. As the divine ideas are exemplar causes of created essences, they are the causes of the principle of potency (which requires a principle of act); the divine nature on the other hand is the exemplar cause of any act of being, and thus the cause of the principle of act (which requires a principle of limitation). The distinction, then, is *real*, but entails no composition or separation in God; furthermore the distinction is necessary to give an account of the world according to Aquinas's Neoplatonic ontology. Both modes of exemplarism are required, and, as Doolan states, "both are dependent upon the mediation of the divine will, for an exemplar is effective only because an agent determines the end of that which is exemplified."[21]

---

[19] Ibid.
[20] Ibid., 243.
[21] Ibid.

The world is, then, the dynamic self-communication of God. That part of the world which can rationally grasp this is intended to be, we can suppose, that to which this divine communication is directed. The world comes forth, and is at every given moment held in existence, by the one from whom it comes, so that marveling at it, and contemplating it, we might come to know something of Him.

The Five Ways

In one of his works on natural theology, Clarke argues that the Five Ways of Aquinas "do not . . . represent the best of St. Thomas's own truly original and most characteristic metaphysical structure of ascent to God as shown in the rest of his works."[22] I have been arguing for this view throughout this book. I began by arguing that the specific reception of Aquinas since the Thomistic revival of the nineteenth century (initiated by the 1879 Leonine encyclical *Aeterni Patris*) has led to the Five Ways being mistakenly understood as a concise presentation of Thomas's own natural theology.[23] I have subsequently sought to demonstrate that the Thomistic project expresses a much richer Platonic ontology, which not only posits God as the necessary explanation for the existence of contingent being, but sees the latter as conveying in part the inner life of the former. I will now return to the Five Ways,

[22] W. Norris Clarke, S.J., *The Philosophical Approach to God* (New York: Fordham University Press, 2007), 42.

[23] Many notable scholars maintain the primacy of the Five Ways for understanding Aquinas's natural theology, and there may indeed be more scope and depth to the Five Ways than Clarke and his followers recognize. Lawrence Dewan, O.P., has argued that the entirety of Thomistic metaphysics can be unfolded out of the Five Ways, including the Neoplatonic themes which are my focus. The debate among Thomists continues.

consider their significance, and situate them where I believe they stand in the philosophy of Aquinas.[24]

The first Way is an argument from motion, meaning the actualization of some potentiality. The cause of this actualization cannot be in the thing itself as there would be no explanation as to why it was not already in act: "Nothing can be reduced from potentiality to actuality except by something in a state of actuality." For example, fire, which is actually hot, makes wood, which only has the potentiality to be hot, become actually hot.

"Whatever is in motion must be put in motion by another," but whatever puts that object in motion must itself have been put in motion by another, and so on. If this regression were to go on to infinity, there would obviously be no First Mover, and there could not then intelligibly be any "subsequent movers." It follows that the existence of an Unmoved First Mover is *necessary*, "and this everyone understands to be God."

It may be argued that animals are not put in motion by something extrinsic, but are *self-moving*. Loosely speaking, animals move themselves. Strictly speaking, however, animals are put in motion because one part of the animal moves the other: a dog's legs move due to the flexing of muscles, which flex due to a release of salt solution, in turn triggered by certain moving motor neurons and so forth. The movement of a "self-moving" object, when considered in detail, must be traced back to an Unmoved First Mover for any explanation.

The Mover, then, is immediately and intrinsically involved in all operations in the universe at any given time, and therefore this Way concludes to a theistic notion of God, and not a

---

[24] All quotations without citation in this section are taken from *Summa Theo.* I, 2, 3.

deistic one. God, here, does not set the universe in motion and leave it to operate like a machine; as Aristotle notes, "when a thing moves because it is moved, the mover and the mobile object are moved simultaneously."[25] For example, we can imagine a man's hand moving a wooden staff, and the staff moving a pebble, which in turn has upon it a leaf. It is true to say that the hand is what is moving the staff, and the staff is what moves the pebble, and the pebble the leaf. But it is also true to say that the hand moves all three objects.

The Unmoved Mover then is "unmoved" because its existence need not be actualized by anything preceding it in the order of being. Therefore, the Unmoved Mover is Pure Act, its essence being to exist (it "just is"): the Necessary First Being.

The second Way begins with asserting the fact that "the senses reveal to us an order of efficient causes."[26] Nothing however can be the cause of itself, as then "it would be prior to itself, which is impossible." In a series of efficient causes, the first cause is the cause of the intermediate causes, which are themselves the cause of the endmost cause. If there were no first cause, there could be no subsequent causes; an infinite regress is impossible, so "it is necessary to admit a first efficient cause, to which everyone gives the name God."

It may seem that there is no real difference between the First and Second Ways, except a semantic one: *Unmoved Mover* and *Uncaused Cause*. The fundamental difference is well explained by Feser:

> Whereas the First Way is concerned to explain why things undergo change, the Second Way is intended to

[25] *Physics* VII, 2, 892.
[26] Feser, *Aquinas*, 81.

explain why they exist at all, where (as in the First Way) the causal influence of the first cause is not something that occurred merely at some point in the past, but which exists here and now. That is to say, just as the First Way is meant to show that no motion or change would occur here and now unless there was a first unmoved mover operating here and now, the Second Way is meant to show that nothing would even exist here and now unless there were a first uncaused cause sustaining things in being here and now.[27]

As we have shown throughout, in all contingent things essence and existence are *really* distinct principles. The second Way is seeking to answer the question of how a thing's essence is then conjoined with its *act of existing* that it may indeed be a real thing, i.e., how a thing comes to be.

Nothing contingent can bring itself into existence because nothing can precede itself. Therefore it is "necessary that everything whose act of existing is other than its nature have its act of existing from another . . . there must then be something which causes all things to exist, inasmuch as it is subsistent existence alone."[28] That which is "subsistent existence alone" is that which has an essence identical with its existence: God. With this Way, the classic objection, "If everything has a cause, God too must have a cause" can be dismissed as a *non sequitur*. It is only things that do not have existence as their essence that need a cause.

It is not enough however that the act of existence and essence of an object are merely conjoined; they "must be *kept*

---

[27] Ibid., 84.
[28] *De Ente et Essentia* V.

together at every point at which the thing exists."[29] If that which kept essence and existence conjoined in any given thing were itself a composite of those same principles, we would have an infinite regress rendering all things unintelligible; therefore that which keeps all things in existence must have an essence identical with its existence, i.e., the Necessary First Being.

These first two Ways enable the philosopher to avoid the counterintuitive infinite regress by offering two paths by which one can follow causal chains back to an uncaused Cause. This Cause is arguably not the same as an absolute *Source*, which would explain not only the existence of finite beings, but *why* the world is as it is.

The third Way argues from the fact that things are generated and corrupted—they come into existence and cease to exist—but "that which is possible not to be at some time is not." That is, if it is possible for a thing not to exist, given infinite time, at some point it did not exist.

From the premise (if accepted), the argument continues as follows: Anything that has an essence distinct from its existence does not have a necessary existence; therefore as it can be said of everything that it is possible not to exist, at some point it did not exist. If there was a time then when nothing existed then nothing would exist now, for the basic reason that "that which does not exist only begins to exist by something already existing." Therefore "there must be something the existence of which is necessary" and so "having of itself its own necessity, and not receiving it from another, but rather causing in others their necessity." Put simply, the world of things, whether having contingent natures or necessary ones,

[29] Feser, *Aquinas*, 85.

could not exist at all unless there were a being whose essence is identical with its existence, i.e., a First Being existing of itself, with no cause of its existence.

Clarke rejects the third Way entirely on the grounds that this is one of the rare occasions in which Aquinas takes for his point of departure an invalid premise, namely that given infinite time, all possibilities will be realized.[30] It is equally plausible that each contingent being should generate another before itself corrupting, and for a process of this kind to continue forever, there being no intrinsic relationship between the notion of infinite time and the realization of every possibility.[31]

Clarke believes that most Thomists agree with him that the third Way does not stand up to scrutiny, but he suggests that few are truly honest about this.[32] Most of these scholars, he submits, opt for the seemingly similar—but much briefer—argument in the *Summa Contra Gentiles* (I, 15, 5), whilst insisting that this substitution is only for the purposes of simplicity and brevity. In fact, according to Clarke, this argument "proceeds on an entirely different principle requiring no recourse at all to the principle that all possibilities must come true, given infinite time."[33]

I shall move immediately to the fifth Way, addressing the fourth last. The fifth Way is especially helpful in demonstrat-

[30] See Clarke, *The Philosophical Approach*, 42–44.

[31] It is plausible that Clark misunderstands Aquinas's argument. For a different interpretation and account of the Third Way, see Lawrence Dewan, O.P., *The Distinctiveness of St. Thomas's "Third Way,"* https://www.cambridge.org/core/journals/dialogue-canadian-philosophical-review-revue-canadienne-de-philosophie/article/distinctiveness-of-st-thomas-third-way/0952638654074E7CBAB5D4678BF6AA16.

[32] Clarke, *The Philosophical Approach*, 44.

[33] Ibid.

ing how the order of the world, with each being innately directed toward achieving its *telos*, indicates the existence of something which is itself limited by no potentiality. The argument is as follows: We observe that "things which lack intelligence, such as natural bodies, act for an end, and this is evident from their acting always, or nearly always, in the same way, so as to obtain the best result." It is clear that such things act "not fortuitously, but designedly," as that which lacks intelligence can act for an end only if it is directed by something which has intelligence. "Therefore some intelligent being exists by whom all natural things are directed to their end; and this being we call God."

Most so-called "design" arguments for the existence of God are variations on the "watchmaker" argument, but the watchmaker analogy lends itself to a deist conception of God.[34] Aquinas's "design" argument, however, as I will explain, presents a solely theistic notion of God's existence. Not only does the watchmaker analogy suggest that God's existence is only very probable, as opposed to necessary, but it also advances a more Newtonian mechanistic conception of the world quite different from that proposed by Aquinas.

Final causation is an intelligibility we see in the world around us, namely, goal-directedness. An acorn, when in the

---

[34] Famously formulated by William Paley in his work *Natural Theology or Evidence of the Existence and Attributes of the Deity* (1802), Paley's argument can be summarized as the following: If one found a beautiful timepiece—and had never seen one before—one would see how well it works, with all the little pieces affecting one another, and conclude that it was the fruit of another person's genius, and that it is only reasonable to presume that it did not just come about by chance. Paley then argues that the same too can be said of the universe, that it is reasonable to suggest that someone made it, and if so that must be God.

necessary environment, becomes an oak tree, and only ever an oak tree:

> The fact that A regularly brings about B, as B's *efficient* cause, entails that bringing about B is in turn the *final* cause of A. For if we did not suppose that A inherently "points to" or is "directed towards" the generation of B as its natural end, then we would have no way to account for the fact that A typically does generate *B* specifically, rather than C, or D, or E, or indeed rather than no effect at all.[35]

Those who argue that all things just happen by chance simply self-refute, for the notion of chance itself presupposes causal regularity.

Now, a horseshoe can be made by a blacksmith because it is preceded by an idea in the intellect of the blacksmith. The horseshoe is itself the final cause of the blacksmith's actions, the actions being the efficient cause. For a cause to have any efficacy it must in some way exist, and if that existence is not extramental then it can only be in the intellect. As non-intellectual beings act for an end, an extrinsic intellect must direct them. We therefore need a divine intellect which does not itself need to be acted upon (thus "divine"). This divine intellect is not merely involved in the genesis of the world, but also must be *here and now*, because causes are *here and now*.

The "final cause is the cause of the other causes," for it *determines* all causes.[36] For a thing to have a final cause, it must also have a formal and material cause, and so a certain

---

[35] Feser, *Aquinas*, 113.

[36] Thomas Aquinas, *Commentary on Aristotle's Physics*, II, 5, 186, trans. Richard J. Blackwell, Richard J. Spath, and W. Edmund Thirkel (London: Routledge and Kegan Paul, 1963).

essence or nature, and this must be so, otherwise it would not be capable of realizing its finality. For "upon the form follows an inclination to the end . . . for everything, in so far as it is in act, acts and tends towards that which is in accordance with its form." However, whatever the object in question is, it must have an essence conjoined with its existence. This in turn can be brought about, and maintained, only by something outside and preceding it; and ultimately that something must not depend on another for this, and so must have an essence identical with its existence. It follows then that whatever orders things to their ends must also be the cause of those things, and so Pure Act, i.e., the First Being, having necessity of itself. Again, like the first two Ways, the fifth Way only gets us so far as to affirm a First Cause, which is, as we have said, not enough to account for what is meant by an absolute Source. Nonetheless, this Way establishes the First Cause as *final* as well as *efficient* cause of the world.

I have left the fourth Way till the end on the grounds that it appears to be the closest to the Neoplatonically inspired natural theology which I claim to be Aquinas's own. The argument begins by acknowledging that "among beings there are some more and some less good, true, noble, and the like," just as "a thing is said to be hotter according as it more nearly resembles that which is hottest." There must, then, be "something which is truest, something best, something noblest, and, consequently, something which is uttermost being; for those things that are greatest in truth are greatest in being." In any case, we intuit a hierarchy of being even before we reason it through, for we know that a log tumbling off a cliff is not as grave as a dog tumbling off a cliff, and that is not as serious as a human being tumbling off. Each is a higher substance than the other.

One objection to this Way is that if God were the most good, true, and noble being, he would also be the "perfect maximum of conceivable smelliness," or indeed the maximum of any attribute.[37] This in fact would not be the case as it is not the *accidental predicates*, only attributed to *particular* beings, which need explaining by reference to what is understood by Aquinas to be God. He is instead concerned with the attributes of being *in general*, those "transcendental attributes" which are called such because they are above every genus and common to every being, "unrestricted to any particular category or individual."[38] In turn, to the extent that these attributes of *being* come in degrees, they must be traceable to a maximum. The transcendental attributes are the attributes of substance *per se*, not accidents of particular beings. Furthermore, as we have said, these attributes are held by Aquinas to be convertible with one another, i.e., they are all one but differing in aspect.

In inquiring into the transcendental attributes we can "start by considering the natures of each of the lower levels of reality and then proceed to follow them upward, [and then] we find ourselves inexorably led to a highest level."[39] The transcendental attributes all point beyond themselves to a highest degree of each, and due to their convertibility, must culminate in one same single maximum. As attributes of being in general, this "single maximum" must be that which is most fully real, i.e., what *is* absolute. We are not simply looking at a hierarchy of things topping one another, one

---

[37] Richard Dawkins, *The God Delusion* (London: Transworld Publishers, 2007), 102.

[38] Feser, *Aquinas*, 105.

[39] Ibid., 107.

after the other, but rather a hierarchy of being in general. This is indeed an argument from *participation*, for something participates in a certain perfection when it possesses that perfection in a potential and limited way. Furthermore, there is an essential link between *participating* in something and being *efficiently caused* by it, for "whatever is found in anything by participation, must be caused in it by that to which it belongs essentially." That, then, in which *particular beings* participate is *being* in general (*esse commune*), which must exist by that which does not itself participate anything, i.e., the Necessary First Being, *ipsum esse per se subsistens*.

This argument pithily outlines what we have described as "participation in the likeness of the divine essence" or "exemplarism of the divine nature." It is an argument from *participation*; one that moves from the transcendental attributes predicated of finite beings to the being (*actus essendi*) of those beings, and from that to contingent being *per se* (*esse commune*), then proceeding to that which accounts for being *per se*, namely God (*esse subsistens*). Again, by this we arrive at a Necessary First Being and Cause, but not to a discovery of the divine ideas. The unique contribution of Aquinas is that of the principle of *esse* in a way that unites Aristotelian realism with the Neoplatonic notion of emanation of the divine ideas in the realization of created essence.

In turn, how are we to situate the Five Ways, if they are not a full summary of Aquinas's own natural theology? Clarke places the Five Ways in Aquinas's wider schema, and thereby answers this question in the following way:

> The Five Ways [should be understood] as quick, condensed sketches of philosophical approaches to God, laid down by St. Thomas at the beginning of his *Summa*

Theologica—intended for "beginners," by the way, as he tells us—deliberately not taken from his own personal participation metaphysics but drawn from the thought of pagan philosophers, especially the newly introduced Aristotle, *the* philosopher for Thomas and so many in his day, for the express purpose of showing that even the pagan philosophers could by the use of reason alone arrive at an initial knowledge of God. After this first step, St. Thomas comes in with his own more high-powered metaphysics.[40]

Taken together, the Five Ways offer a path to God open to all who philosophically distance themselves from the world in order to contemplate it and reflect upon it. This can be described in three mental steps. Firstly, all beings of our experience lack their own reason for existing, and require some cause to explain their existence. An infinite regress of causes would fail to explain proximate causes, and so fail to explain the beings of our experience. Hence, there must be one being whose essence it is to exist. Secondly, such a being must be unlimited and infinite, otherwise its limitation would require explanation, i.e., "it would have to pre-exist its own being and choose for itself this particular limited degree of perfection rather than another—which is impossible."[41] If every finite being requires a cause to explain its existence, that which has no cause must be infinite in perfection. Thirdly, there can only be one infinitely perfect being; for were there more, the others would be distinct only by some limitation and finitude. Hence, there is one infinite and perfect cause of the world.

---

[40] Clarke, *The Philosophical Approach*, 45.
[41] Ibid.

The argument I present is that Aquinas's own natural theology takes us further still. In turn, the one qualification I would wish to make to the extended quotation from Clarke above is that the fourth Way does in part introduce us to Aquinas's "own personal participation metaphysics," moving us, via the world around us, in an ascent all the way to, ultimately, a theory of the exemplarism of the divine nature. For this reason Gilson, a near pure Aristotelian, admits that "the fourth Way openly relies upon the validity of the Platonic and Augustinian notion of participation," indicating that "exemplarism is one of the essential elements of St. Thomas's thought."[42] Such a theory should naturally give rise to a theory of exemplarism of divine ideas, these two orders of exemplarism being correlative in the formation of a complete ontology.

---

[42] Etienne Gilson, *The Christian Philosophy of St. Thomas Aquinas* (Indiana: University of Notre Dame Press, 1994), 74.

4

Participation Metaphysics
and Aesthetics

We prefer to be always seeking him through knowledge
and never finding what we seek, rather than to possess
by loving that which would be found in vain without
loving.

—Giovanni Pico della Mirandola,
On Being and the One

The Renaissance and the narrative of discontinuity

VICTORIAN SCHOLARSHIP on the intellectual culture of
the Renaissance, which was probably the consequence of the appreciation of the aesthetic achievements of the Italian Renaissance that had given rise to the
Grand Tour in the previous century, was almost entirely blind
to the central place of Thomism during this period.[1] This
oversight was perhaps helped in part by the scathing remarks
made by scholars from both the south and north during the
Renaissance period, especially Lorenzo Valla and Desiderius
Erasmus, regarding the barbaric form of medieval scholastic
Latin in comparison with classical and patristic Latin. This

---

[1] An obvious example of this is Walter Pater, *Studies in the History of
the Renaissance* (Oxford: Oxford University Press, 1986; first published
in 1873).

93

does not, however, tell us anything about their view of medieval philosophy, only the way in which it was conveyed. Indeed, regarding scholastic ideas themselves, we find almost exclusively comments of praise, and an eagerness to defend and apply the principles of medieval thought. A few examples will suffice to illustrate this.

There were three major centers of philosophical learning during the Renaissance period (roughly mid-14th to mid-16th centuries): that of the Tudor court of England, the city-state courts of the Italian peninsula (especially those of Medici Florence and the Papal States), and the Spanish imperial academies of Salamanca and Valladolid.[2]

Regarding the Tudor court, we may consider three major figures in philosophy: Erasmus, Thomas More, and John Fisher. Erasmus was less a philosopher than a classicist and biblical scholar. However, in his one great work of philosophy, namely his 1524 response to Luther on the nature of free will entitled *De libero arbitrio diatriba*, he holds to a deeply Thomistic anthropology.

With good reason Jacques Maritain referred to More as a "bon disciple de saint Thomas d'Aquin."[3] The Thomism of More has often been neglected by scholars, but Samuel Gregg points out that More was influenced by the thought of

---

[2] There were many more centers of Renaissance humanism, including those in the northern lowlands, Bohemia, Hungary, Transylvania, Poland, and its neighboring Grand Duchy of Lithuania. Nevertheless, the three posts of England, Italy, and Spain were indisputably the major *philosophical* centers of the Renaissance.

[3] Jacques Maritain, "La Philosophie du Droit," in *The King's Good Servant: Papers Read to the Thomas More Society of London*, ed. Richard O'Sullivan (Oxford: Basil Blackwell, 1941), 41.

Aquinas in three key areas: faith and reason, philosophical anthropology, and political philosophy:

> Thomistic thought informs crucial elements of More's contribution to crucial debates—specifically discussions concerning the relationship between faith and reason, the character of the will (especially its place vis-à-vis reason), and the place of equity in the workings of judicial systems—that shaped the social, political and legal landscape of sixteenth-century Europe.[4]

More referred to the "Angelic Doctor" as "the flower of theology, and a man of that true and perfect faith."[5] More had been appalled that the word "Thomistic" had been used by Luther as a pejorative term.[6] No doubt his defense of Aquinas's thought was at least in part a response to Tyndale's claim that bringing philosophy into theological reflection was gravely mistaken.[7] More had even used Thomistic epistemology in his apologetics, suggesting that the relationship between mental images, or "phantasmata," and the immaterial intelligence be considered as an analogue of the pious Christian's use of sacred images and statues.[8] More was not alone as both a humanist and intellectual disciple of Aquinas;

---

[4] Samuel Gregg, "Faith, Reason, and Order," in *Thomas More: Why Patron of Statesmen?*, ed. Travis Curtright (New York: Lexington Books, 2015), 95.

[5] Thomas More, "Confutation of Tyndale's Answer," in *The Complete Works of St. Thomas More* (New Haven: Yale University Press, 1997), VIII, 713.

[6] See More, *The Complete Works*, V, 324.

[7] See William Tyndale, *The Obedience of the Christian Man* (Clermont-Ferrand: Digireads, 2012), art. 154–58.

[8] See Thomas More, *Dialogue Concerning Heresies* (New York: Scepter Publishers, 2006), 60–62.

indeed "Fisher's theology is [also] marked by a . . . far from unsuccessful attempt to reinvigorate the old blood of the scholastics with the new blood of the humanists."[9] Fisher, like More, had described Aquinas as the "most learned and at the same time most holy."[10]

Little needs to be said about the philosophers of Salamanca and Valladolid regarding their Thomism. Indeed, when one considers the key Spanish figures of the Renaissance period, namely Francisco de Vitoria, Domingo de Soto, Francisco Suárez, and Luis de Molina, the task is not so much to prove their commitment to Thomism as to establish their interest in the Renaissance humanist movement. Nevertheless, although it is clear that they were predominantly scholastics, and not humanists, they studied and admired the "new learning," and this is illustrated well by Vitoria's interest in—and sympathy for—"Erasmian humanism" in particular.[11]

In the Florentine court of the Medici, where Lorenzo de' Medici sought to establish a community of scholars, the leading courtier-philosophers were Giovanni Pico della Mirandola and Marsilio Ficino. These two men were humanists *par excellence*, together translating, commenting upon, and developing a broader philosophy from the texts of Plato. These texts had recently arrived from Byzantium due to the Council of Florence and the subsequent scholarly Latin writings about these texts by the Anatolian-born Cardinal Basilios Bessarion. Pico, who is often written about as a pure Platonist,

[9] Richard Rex, *The Theology of John Fisher* (Cambridge: Cambridge University Press, 2003), 1.

[10] Edward Sturz, S.J., *The Works and Days of John Fisher* (Cambridge: Harvard University Press, 1967), 162.

[11] Brian P. Copenhaver & Charles B. Schmitt, *Renaissance Philosophy* (Oxford: Oxford University Press, 2002), 113.

in fact had a profound interest in Aquinas; indeed Pico's famous *Nine-hundred Theses* (issued in 1486) includes forty-five theses explicitly in defense of Aquinas's thought.[12] Ficino, to whom we shall return shortly, was equally an intellectual disciple of Aquinas.

There is an important reason for this brief historical digression. I have argued that there was a warped reception of Aquinas during the Thomistic revival from the end of the nineteenth century, with Aquinas judged as a pure (albeit Christian) Aristotelian, alongside an almost total neglect of his Neoplatonic metaphysics. So too a view has been all too frequently advanced that Renaissance humanism was simply hostile to medieval scholasticism and sought to replace the entire philosophical system which had come before with a new Platonic worldview. This is a way of considering Renaissance philosophy within a narrative of discontinuity analogous to the way many have until recently thought about Aquinas and his use of Aristotle. In fact, in both cases, a deeper study of the primary sources gives rise to a narrative of continuity.

The point here is not that the leading Renaissance thinkers were not really Platonists, but rather that they *were* Platonists. The fact that they were Christian Platonists does not "dovetail" well with their choice for Aquinas as an intellectual master if we accept the narrative of discontinuity view of Aquinas. Aquinas's prestige among the humanists of the Renaissance is simply not accounted for by the received view of Aquinas which my position challenges.

---

[12] See Paul Oskar Kristeller, *Medieval Aspects of Renaissance Learning* (Duke University Press, 1974), 72.

It is of considerable importance that Ficino, after having been commissioned by Lorenzo de' Medici to translate the entire corpus of Plato into Latin, and after writing a complete commentary for his translation, referred to Aquinas's participation metaphysics in his magnum opus. Fabro explains:

> One philosopher who was decidedly on his way to seeing in Thomas the metaphysical tension of act and potency grounded in the notion of participation, was Marsilio Ficino, the prince of Humanism of the *Quattrocento*. In his major work, the *Theologica Platonica*, he acknowledges the principal theses of Thomistic metaphysics and, while recalling the notion of participation, he fights against the triumphant Averroism with the same arguments used by St. Thomas, whom he calls "the bright light of Christian theology." Had his voice been heard, many useless disputes within the orders would have been avoided.[13]

What Fabro highlights here further supports my challenge to the received view of Aquinas. I wish however to go further still, and argue in this final chapter that the consequence of the view of Aquinas which I have presented is that a Platonic *aesthetics* can be accommodated by the Thomistic synthesis. It is my view that Platonism, as it is assumed into the Thomistic project, can be—and has been—applied to all areas of philosophy which proceed either directly or indirectly from Aquinas's ontology. I will, however, focus only on aesthetics due to the widespread appeal of Platonic aesthetics. In turn, I intend to demonstrate how—reframed within Thomism— we can conserve all that makes this theory of aesthetics so

---

[13] Fabro, "The Intensive Hermeneutics," 480.

appealing, whilst elevating it further. This will serve not only to support the wider argument of this thesis, but will demonstrate its application to another category of philosophy beyond pure metaphysics.

I end this section by merely mentioning in passing that those widely considered to be the greatest artists of the Renaissance period, at least of the Italian Renaissance, stayed for some time at the court of the Medici specifically to study under Ficino. These included Michelangelo, Botticelli, da Vinci, Raphael, Brunelleschi, Donatello, Masaccio, Verrocchio, Piero, Uccello, and many more. This list of masters should at least indicate that the Platonic Thomism which Ficino was developing (in his opinion, in continuity with Aquinas's own project) could have profound consequences for the area of aesthetics. A number of these artists explicitly called themselves Platonists, especially the ones who produced some of the most treasured representations of Aquinas. It is obvious that it would be of particular philosophical advantage if Aquinas's ontology could be shown to accommodate the Platonic aesthetics so widely valued.

Platonic aesthetics and Aquinas

The main doctrine of what has come to be known as "Platonic aesthetics" finds its source in the speech made by Socrates at 210a–212c of Plato's *Symposium*, during which Socrates recounts a dialogue concerning love and beauty which he once had with Diotima, a Mantinean philosopher and priestess. The argument contained therein has been highly influential, and runs as follows. The love of a particular beauty, especially the beauty of another's body, ought to move one to admire more generally the beauty of all things apprehended by the senses, above all the beauty of all attractive bodies. Then, in getting to know those who are beautiful in appearance one ought to discover that some possess beautiful minds too, and in turn the love of beauty should transcend the pursuit of beautiful bodies to reach the pursuit of ideas, and therefore beautiful immaterial realities. The beauty of great minds will cause one to love such minds even when found in those not possessing an appearance of particular aesthetic value. Finally, having come to love the laws and principles of reason, one will transcend the world of material objects altogether, to contemplate only the perennial and immaterial realties, and ultimately the perfect undiminished form of beauty itself. As Diotima, through the mouth of Socrates, summarizes:

> Like someone using a staircase, he should go from one to two, and from two to all beautiful bodies, and from beautiful bodies to beautiful practices, and from practices to beautiful forms of learning. From forms of learning, he should end up at that form of learning which is of nothing other than *that* beauty itself, so that he can contemplate the process of learning what beauty really is.[14]

Finally, Diotima claims that such a life of contemplating the form of beauty is the best kind of life, for since there is then some connaturality between the soul of the one who loves beauty and the form of beauty, the latter causes the former itself to be beautiful; and beauty of the soul is called *virtue*: "It is only in that kind of life, when someone sees beauty with the part that can see it, that he will be able to give birth . . . to true virtue."[15]

[14] *Symposium* 211c.
[15] Ibid., 212a.

The broader point here, which is what has had such a long-standing influence, is the notion that what can be known via the senses, when beautiful, may be a way by which we ascend to the contemplation of that which is immaterial. However, Plato is not particularly helpful in regard to the relationship between beauty and art. His main concern is that the beauty of, say, immoral poetry or theatre might corrupt the developing virtue of the young.[16] However much the deliberate coupling of art and beauty was seen as innovative when Hegel's lectures on aesthetics were posthumously published in the nineteenth century, artists have generally sought to avoid ugliness and maximize beauty, and it is natural to think that the concept of art is closely connected to that of beauty.[17] In turn, it understandably strikes us as strange that Plato argues in defense of beauty, and yet maintains such a negative attitude towards art. I will shortly attempt to explain this.

Pseudo-Dionysius, who was intellectually downstream from Plato in being one of many Church Fathers to synthesize the Christian deposit with Neoplatonic metaphysics, developed a way of thinking about beauty specifically in relation to participation metaphysics. Here is an example from the *De Divinis Nominibus*:

> One should distinguish between beauty and beautiful-ness as the cause of embracing at once all beauty. For, having made this distinction in all being between participation and things participating, we call beautiful the thing which participates in beautifulness, because from

---

[16] *Republic*, 376d–410b.

[17] See Monroe C. Beardsley, *Aesthetics: Problems in the Philosophy of Criticism*, 2nd ed. (Indianapolis: Hackett Publishing Company, 1981).

it is imparted to all reality the beauty appropriate to every thing, and also because it is the cause of proportion and brilliance.[18]

The position of Pseudo-Dionysius is clearly derived from Plotinus's view that beauty in the world is "an emanation from Absolute Being."[19] Plotinus's theme "mounts even higher in the Pseudo-Dionysius's indissoluble conjunction of Beauty and the Good as an attribute of God: which is of course conflated with the Neoplatonist Absolute."[20] Pseudo-Dionysius, this great Christian Neoplatonic authority, is one of Aquinas's main sources, quoted more frequently than any other single thinker in the *Summa Theologica*, and so we should not be surprised at his influence on Aquinas's aesthetic understanding.

The Platonic view of beauty presented in the *Symposium* was systematized within a Neoplatonic theory of metaphysical participation, and assumed into the discipline of theology by the Church Fathers, both Latin and Greek. This again became a highly influential current in the medieval period and has shaped Western art and architecture ever since. The Benedictine monastery, the Abbaye de St.-Denis, was named after Dionysius the Areopagite, who converted to Christianity after hearing Paul of Tarsus preach in Athens, during which Paul had shown his knowledge of Hellenistic thought

[18] Quoted in W. Tatarkiewicz, *Medieval Aesthetics*, trans. R. M. Montgomery (The Hague: Mouton, 1970), 33.

[19] Joseph Margolis, "Medieval Aesthetics," in *The Routledge Companion to Aesthetics*, 2nd ed., ed. Berys Gaut and Dominic McIver Lopes (London: Routledge, 2005), 31.

[20] Ibid.

by quoting from memory the Pre-Socratic Epimenides of Cnossos and the third century BC Cilician poet Aratus (Acts 17:16–34). At the time of Abbot Suger (Abbot of the Abbaye de St.-Denis from 1122 to 1151), the biblical Dionysius was thought to be the same person as the writer we refer to as Pseudo-Dionysius, a philosopher and theologian modern scholars place in the late fifth to early sixth centuries. Suger was devoted to the patron saint of the monastery, and studied (what he believed to be) his writings closely. On becoming Abbot, Suger made the decision to deconstruct and rebuild the monastery, an extraordinary and audacious decision as it was a prominent place of pilgrimage and the ancient burial site of the Kings of the Franks. He sought to apply the principles of Platonic aesthetics, as they had been received through the writings of Pseudo-Dionysius, in the rebuilding of his monastery. It was this that marked the move from late Romanesque to early Gothic architecture, a current which would immediately sweep across Western Europe and beyond.

Suger sought to employ the Platonic idea that the beauty of things apprehended by the senses can raise the mind to that which is immaterial—this, as framed by the Neoplatonism of Pseudo-Dionysius, being the Uncreated Beauty from which all things derive their particularized and diminished beauty through emanation and by participation. For Suger this was best expressed by what we today call Gothic: the slender Corinthian pillar, the ribbed vault, the flying buttress, the high steeple or tower, the rose window, and the pointed arch. Suger is at pains to present the connection between these elements and the thought of "St. Denis" in his *Liber de Rebus in Administratione sua Gestis*, *Libellus Alter de Consecratione Ecclesiae Sancti Dionysii*, and the *Ordinatio*; all written while, or soon after, he oversaw the monastery's construction.[21] It should be noted that the Abbaye de St.-Denis was completed in 1144, one hundred and one years before Aquinas began his studies at the University of Paris, located just an hour's pony ride from the Abbaye. Aquinas, I claim, stands in the same tradition of Neoplatonic metaphysics as Abbot Suger, being downstream from the same sources, and this comes out clearly in his approach to questions of aesthetics.

Aquinas remarks that "the notion (*ratio*) of the beautiful is that which calms the desire, by being seen or known."[22] This, however, does not aim at what constitutes beauty, but only what the experience of beauty causes in the one subject to it. In turn, Aquinas's statement here "is to introduce the problem, not to solve it."[23] It is at the level of the transcendental attributes, and therefore at the level of participation, that Aquinas seeks to present what actually constitutes beauty. For Aquinas, beauty has an *essential* relationship with the transcendental attributes of *being*. He explains this by stating that there are three components which, when seized by the human intelligence, enable us to judge beauty:

> Beauty includes three conditions, integrity or perfection, since those things which are impaired are by the very fact ugly; due proportion or harmony; and lastly, brightness or clarity, whence things are called beautiful which have a bright color.[24]

---

[21] This topic is covered in great detail in Erwin Panofsky, *On the Abbey Church of St.-Denis and Its Art Treasures* (Princeton: Princeton University Press, 1979).

[22] *Summa Theo.* I-II, 27, 1.

[23] Umberto Eco, *Art and Beauty in the Middle Ages* (London: Yale University Press, 1986), 128.

[24] *Summa Theo.* I, 39, 8.

The three "conditions" which Aquinas mentions are in fact understood to be transcendental attributes of *being* as grasped through the prism of aesthetics. I summaries these in the following three paragraphs:

1) Integrity (*Integritas*): This is what conveys the reality of the thing, the radiance of the form, the whole having all its parts intact and in their collective fullness. It communicates that the individuated object conforms well to its universal nature. We understand that it is beautiful because we see that it is *good*, i.e., it has integrity: it is—and is seen to be—the sort of thing it is supposed to be.

2) Proportion (*Consonantia*): By this condition we grasp the order and *unity* of the object, particularly how it is ordered toward its finality. Augustine anticipates this idea when he writes that "everything is beautiful that is in due order."[25] In the case of a human being, for example, if he is disproportionately given over to pleasure, and so does not have temperance, kindness, self-regard, etc. he becomes an existential ugliness, and loses the admiration of others. Or, visually, if a dog has a disproportionate body in relation to its legs it will be ugly, or at best comical, but not beautiful. On the other hand if a dog is well proportioned, he is judged a well-structured creature and pleasing to look upon.

3) Clarity (*Claritas*): By this condition the object is understood, its intelligibility is seized. The object is beautiful because it reveals its ontological reality clearly, and the *truth* of it is known. It is via this condi-

[25] Augustine of Hippo, *Of True Religion*, XLI, 77, trans. J. H. S. Burleigh (Chicago: Henry Regnery Company, 1959).

tion that we can not only answer the question of "what is it?" but answer this question with precision. For example, when we look at Bernini's *Ecstasy of Saint Teresa* we can clearly see exactly what the sculpture is seeking to convey: the *truth* of it is known. The object is deemed beautiful because the truth of it is easily grasped by the intelligence.

These three conditions are convertible with one another precisely because they are the transcendental attributes of being understood through the prism of the beautiful, with which they are also convertible.[26] This of course logically means that

[26] Recently the scholastic notion of the convertibility of certain principles has made its way into the writings of Analytic philosophers in the ideas of intensionality and hyperintensionality. In brief: the extension of a term is the set of things it refers to; for example, the extension of the term "creature with a heart" is the set of all creatures that have hearts. On the other hand, the intension of a term is a function that takes us from a particular situation to the set of things it refers to (its extension) in that situation. Intensions can be useful for explaining the difference in meaning between two terms that have the same extension. For example "creature with a heart" has the same extension as "creature with a kidney" because as it happens all creatures that have hearts have kidneys and vice versa. But "creature with a heart" does not *mean* the same thing as "creature with a kidney." And we can explain this by saying that they have different intensions: the function from "creature with a heart" to its extension actually yields the same set of things as the function from "creature with a kidney" to its extension. But we can imagine situations in which it *would not*. An Analytic philosopher may wonder, if transcendentals like "beauty" and "being" are convertible, that must mean it is impossible for something to have one without the other; but in that case the intension of "beauty" and the intension of "being" will be the same (in every possible situation the set of beautiful things is identical to the set of beings), and this cannot be the case as the meaning of "beauty" is clearly different from the meaning of "being" (i.e. they are not "conceptually identical"). The answer, in contemporary Analytic parlance, is that "beauty," "being," and words for other transcendentals are *hyperinten-*

ugliness is not some-*thing*, but a privation of being; ugliness has the character of evil. In turn, whatever *is* is beautiful, and in the hierarchy of being whatever most *is* is uttermost beauty.

Roger Scruton raises a problem regarding the convertibility of beauty with truth, and beauty with goodness. He argues that "goodness and truth never compete . . . the pursuit of one is always compatible with a proper respect for the other. The pursuit of beauty, however, is far more questionable."[27] As we have said, the opposition of truth and beauty, as well as goodness and beauty, goes back to Plato. For Plato, art can easily lead people away from the truth, because such representations are "far removed from the truth."[28] So too, art might "produce in the youth a strong inclination to do bad things."[29] It certainly appears to be true that the pursuit of beauty can conflict with the pursuit of both truth and goodness. We can easily be charmed by the beauty of a lie and, believing it, fail to conclude to the truth; and one need only think of the moral ruination of King David from his attraction to the beauty of Bathsheba (2 Samuel 11).

sional, that is, their meaning is not exhausted by their intensions—by the function from a situation to their referents. Another example of hyperintensional terms is "has a shape" and "has a size"; it is not possible to have a shape and not a size, or to have a size and not a shape, but "has a shape" does not mean the same thing as "has a size." There will no doubt be examples of no overlap between the uses of "hyperintensionality" and "convertibility," but there can certainly be said to be an analogue here which may allow for dialogue between the two traditions of Analytic philosophy and Scholastic realism. For a helpful analysis of these terms and their application to metaphysics, see Daniel Nolan, "Hyperintensional Metaphysics," in *Philosophical Studies: An International Journal for Philosophy in the Analytic Tradition* 171.1 (2014): 149–60.

[27] Roger Scruton, *Beauty* (Oxford: Oxford University Press, 2009), 3.

[28] *Republic*, 598b5.

[29] *Republic*, 391e.

Scruton presents it as evident that the pursuit of truth is never in opposition to the pursuit of goodness, or vice versa. But it is not obvious that this is correct. What of someone who lies to accomplish a good, like protecting an innocent person from an injustice? Or the case of someone who carries out a terrorist act in order to bring international attention to the truth regarding the plight of their people?

In fact, Aquinas, who holds that the "beautiful is the same as the good, and they differ in aspect only," fully acknowledges that we are attracted by the good, both real *and apparent*.[30] Concrete situations and persons can mark an admixture of the intelligible good and the unintelligible absence of that reality of the good. In the example of King David and Bathsheba, her physical beauty was truly both real and good, but this acknowledgement does not mitigate the evil, and in turn the *ugliness*, of the betrayal of self and other in the act of adultery (and, in this case, murder too).

Beauty, according to Aquinas, is *conceptually* different and distinct from goodness, but they are *metaphysically* identical. That is to say:

> They differ logically, for goodness properly relates to the appetite (goodness being what all things desire); and therefore it has the aspect of an end (the appetite being a kind of movement towards a thing). On the other hand, beauty relates to the cognitive faculty; for beautiful things are those which please when seen.[31]

As the good, the true, and the beautiful differ in aspect— in how we grasp them—we are able as subjects to intention-

---

[30] *Summa Theo.* I-II, 27, 1.
[31] Ibid., I, 5, 4.

ally *pursue* (to use Scruton's word) one at the expense of the others depending on what aspect we attend to, but that does not mean that they in themselves are not convertible with one another.

Beauty is understood here to be a transcendental attribute. Therefore insofar as something is beautiful, it participates in a likeness of the beauty of the divine nature. This is a point forcefully made by Maritain in the following extended quotation:

> The beautiful belongs to the order of *transcendentals*—that is to say, of concepts which surpass all limits of kind or category and will not suffer themselves to be confined in any class, because they absorb everything and are to be found everywhere. Like the one, the true and the good, it is *being* itself considered from a certain aspect, it is a property of being: it is not an accident superadded to being, it adds to being merely a relation of reason, it is being considered as delighting, by the mere intuition of it, an intellectual nature. So everything is beautiful as everything is good, at least in a certain relation. And as being is everywhere present and everywhere various, the beautiful likewise is scattered everywhere and everywhere various. Like being and the other transcendentals, it is essentially *analogous*, that is to say it is predicated for diverse reasons, *sub diversa ratione*, of the diverse subjects of which it is predicated: each kind of being *is* in its own way, is good in its own way, is *beautiful* in its own way. . . . Analogous concepts are properly predicable only of God, in whom the perfection they describe exists in a "formal-eminent" manner, in a pure and infinite state. God is their "sovereign analogue," and they are to be found in things only as a

scattered and prismatised reflection of the face of God.
So Beauty is one of the divine attributes.[32]

Maritain is here presenting a view of beauty which is not
from Aquinas's Aristotelian side, so to speak; clearly the
notion that "the beauty of the world is an image and reflection of Ideal Beauty is Platonic in origin."[33] Maritain's view
of beauty, following Aquinas, is at root a view derived from a
Neoplatonic emanation and participation metaphysics.[34]

When it comes to relating beauty and *art*, Aquinas appears
to do exactly what he does in his metaphysics, i.e., he syn-
thesizes the Platonic and Aristotelian approaches: "Aquinas's
treatment of the beautiful follows the lead of the Pseudo-
Dionysius and Augustine and tends toward the Neoplatonist
conception, whereas his treatment of art . . . tends to favour
Aristotle's discussion of *technê*."[35] *Technê* in this context is the
proper function of the artist, namely the transference of a
new form to matter predisposed to receive it. Aquinas, then,
brings together a broadly Platonic approach to beauty and an
Aristotelian approach to art in order to produce a single
(albeit implicit) theory of aesthetics.

[32] Jacques Maritain, *Art and Scholasticism* (London: Sheed and Ward, 1930), 30.

[33] Eco, *Art and Beauty*, 17.

[34] E.g., Dionysius the Areopagite, *The Divine Names*, trans. C.E. Holt (London: n.p., 1920), 95–96: "The Superessential Beautiful is called 'Beauty' because of that quality which It imparts to all things severally according to their nature, and because It is the Cause of the harmony and splendour in all things, flashing forth upon them all, like light, the beau-tifying communications of Its originating ray; and because It summons all things to fare unto Itself (from whence It hath the name of 'Fairness'), and because It draws all things together in a state of mutual interpenetration."

[35] Margolis, "Medieval Aesthetics," in *The Routledge Companion*, 35.

Those attracted by Platonic aesthetics tend to suppose that it affords a compelling account of the value of artworks, and of the discipline of art in general. Works of art, as objects of beauty—deliberately made to be beautiful—can draw us beyond the works themselves to some transcendent reality. As noted, it is therefore troubling for those attracted to the Platonic account of beauty that Plato himself is so negative about art. Perhaps this is because Plato did not combine his theory of beauty with the theory of art as *technê* which Aristotle advances. This, however, is what Aquinas achieves by bringing into his single ontology both approaches. The result is an appealing account of aesthetic appreciation of art that is uniquely Thomistic in its synthesis of Platonic and Aristotelian elements. Aquinas, however, did not produce a single work on the topic of aesthetics, or art, and passages in his writings which pertain to this, scattered throughout his works, would be brought together and developed into a coherent Thomistic aesthetics only by the twentieth century Neo-Scholastics. In any case, there is a sense in which by synthesizing Platonic aesthetics, as received in Patristic Neoplatonic theology, with the Aristotelian notion of *technê*, Aquinas realized in philosophy what Suger had realized in stone and glass.

The fundamental Aristotelian point in Aquinas's notion of art is that the term *technê* denotes "the imposition of an intelligible form on natural materials (which lack that form) by the work of practical reason."[36] Unlike the beauty of the things of nature, whose beauty points beyond to Uncreated Beauty, art—resulting from the intentionality of the author—presents itself as an *end*, incarnating that very

---

[36] Ibid., 34.

beauty toward which all natural beauties point. Maritain conveys this idea in the following way:

> The work which involves the labour of the Fine Arts is ordered to beauty: insofar as it is beautiful it is an end, an absolute, self-sufficient; and if, as work to be done, it is material and enclosed in a kind, as beautiful it belongs to the realm of the spirit and dives deep into the transcendence and the infinity of being.[37]

The matter, then, which receives the imposed form, will express that form insofar as it is qualitatively appropriate, but this is only a secondary consideration, for it is not the matter which is the primary object of apprehension in the case of art, but the form, i.e., the beauty of art *is* the radiance of the form, at the service of which is the matter. The beauty, then, is situated in the transcendent idea, of which the art (by virtue of its form) is a likeness. For this reason Aquinas "fixes the condition of objective beauty by reference to the perceivable or cognizable form of the things in question."[38]

Art ought not to be confused with record-keeping, as in a courtroom sketch or a group photograph at a birthday party. These cases are quite different from works of art, even when such works have as their subject historical events; this is because art unveils something *universal* in human experience (or at least universally attainable) which is irreducible to this or that particular event. The degree to which a work of art achieves this—and an important part of this will be how the content is expressed due to the mastery involved in realizing the form—is the degree to which we might call it a "master-

---

[37] Maritain, *Art and Scholasticism*, 30.
[38] Margolis, "Medieval Aesthetics," in *The Routledge Companion*, 36.

piece." Essentially, this is to transcend the particular and ascend to that which is universally shared, that is, it is to seize and incarnate that which exemplifies in the divine mind the created realities we behold. In turn, inasmuch as the artist achieves the impression and incarnation of the form, the object exemplifies the *divine mind*; and insofar as this is achieved via the perfecting of the matter in its submission to the imposed form, the object will be beautiful, and so exemplify the *divine nature*.

From this synthetic Aristotelian-Platonic perspective, one begins to see that the vocations of artist and philosopher have the same content. Both the artist and the philosopher must ascend via the created hierarchy to the divine mind, so as to "return to those in the Cave," so to speak, bearing the torch of hidden truth, that it may be seen clearly and brightly. The way by which the philosopher achieves this is to write and speak of what he has seen with the mind's eye; whereas the artist must incarnate in the world that which he has apprehended. Maritain appears to have concluded with a similar view:

> There is a curious analogy between the Fine Arts and wisdom. Like wisdom, they are ordered to an object transcending man and of value in itself, whose fullness is without limit, for beauty is as infinite as being. They are disinterested, pursued for their own sake, truly noble because their work considered in itself is not made to be used as a means, but to be enjoyed as an end, being a true fruit, *aliquid ultimum et delectabile*. Their whole value is spiritual and their manner of being is contemplation. For if contemplation is not their activity, as it is the activity of wisdom, their object is nevertheless to produce an intellectual delight, that is to say a kind of contemplation, and they also presup-

pose in the artist a kind of contemplation, whence the beauty of the work ought to overflow.[39]

It might be said that the artist and the philosopher, in their complementarity, fulfil two divisions of a single vocation. Together they establish paths to a single end: the contemplation of eternal truth. Aquinas seems to have perceived something of this, noting that "the philosopher is likened to the poet, for both concern themselves with that at which we wonder."[40] This notion finds expression in Raphael's *The School of Athens*, in which many of the philosophers depicted bear the faces of great artists and architects of the Italian Renaissance.

The artist intuits the twofold exemplarism of existent beings, and via them reaches up into the mind of God, contemplating the divine mysteries, and in turn brings down into the world the eternal idea which he has seized and made his own, impressing it on the material world in an act of elegant domination. All the while he maximizes the beauty of the form as it is incarnated, applying his sharp technique and prudentially selecting the matter best suited to the work, that the object may exemplify the (convertible) divine mind and nature, affirming the truth of our existence, and testifying to our ultimate end.

The aesthetic experience and the religious experience

The wider ontology I advance, and the specific way the view of aesthetics above follows from it, accounts for the widely felt intuition that there is some deep connection between the aesthetic experience and the religious experience. We have

---

[39] Maritain, *Art and Scholasticism*, 34.
[40] *In I Met.* lect. 1.3, no. 4.

gone some way toward explaining this by a consideration of beauty as a transcendental attribute, and therefore a divine attribute, and of how this can be brought into the discussion of the fine arts. I wish now to make this point more explicitly, with a view to advancing the bold claim that all art (by which I specifically mean the *arts of the beautiful*), without exception, is religious.

By the *fine arts* I mean artworks that express a civilization, and therefore belong to *high culture*. Obviously the concept of a civilization is hard to pin down, but I assume we have a sufficient grasp of the term for the present purposes. In any case, the notions of civilization and high culture go hand-in-hand; the latter is the expression of the former, and the former is defined by its ability to produce the latter.[41] Furthermore, it has been argued that high culture is "downstream" from the religious current of the civilization in question.[42] If this is correct, it should not surprise us that the religious and aesthetic experiences are widely felt to be closely related. Scruton has argued that high culture, although it is efficiently caused by some religious deposit, once it comes into being no longer has any *intrinsic* dependence on its religious origin: "Religion may wither and festivals decline without destroying high culture."[43] It is not clear that history will support this position, however, and many

[41] Although we often call instances of grave immorality "barbaric," this is an equivocation, for it is not primarily morality which distinguishes the civilized from the "barbarian" society. Indeed, civilizations are called such despite their serious moral failings.

[42] See T. S. Eliot, *Notes Towards the Definition of Culture* (London: Faber and Faber, 1962), 26–34.

[43] Roger Scruton, *An Intelligent Person's Guide to Modern Culture* (South Bend, IN: St. Augustine's Press, 2000), 39.

thinkers have taken the view that the separation of art and religion has resulted in the rapid worsening of both. According to T. S. Eliot, the view that "culture can be preserved, extended and developed in the absence of religion" is an "error," but Eliot offers no clear metaphysical reasons for this, opting rather for historical and sociological arguments.[44] Supposing that Eliot's rather than Scruton's view is correct, the metaphysics presented in the above sections provides a specific view of the artistic act that explains why the artist, in no longer seeking to ascend to the divine, has emptied his vocation of its proper content.

Art can be categorized under the headings of the sacred, the pious, and the profane. Sacred art is art "put aside" for holy purposes, namely for the context of the sacred space typically and to play some part in liturgical or ritualistic acts; examples include Velazquez's *Christ Crucified* or Thomas Tallis's composition, the *Mass for four voices*. Pious art is explicitly and consciously religious, but in no way intended for holy service; examples would be Caravaggio's *Salome with the Head of John the Baptist* (either one) or Elgar's *The Dream of Gerontius*, or indeed the original poem of that name by John Henry Newman. Profane art is secular in content and meant entirely for secular purposes, like Vermeer's *The Wine Glass*, the equestrian oil paintings of George Stubbs, or Mozart's *Don Giovanni*.

These kinds of art differ in type rather than degree, due to their particular self-contained ends, and so too our response to their destruction differs in type, rather than degree, but always analogously. What I mean is that even though the act of destroying a work of profane art is not, in the strict sense,

---

[44] Eliot, *Notes Towards the Definition*, 30.

an act of desecration, our response is likely to be similar to our response at the destruction of a sacred work, and of a type that is different—but analogous—to our response in the latter case. Whether it is Michelangelo's *Pietà* or first edition prints of Goya's war scenes being deliberately damaged (as indeed both have been in 1972 and 2001 respectively), our response remains some sort of intense indignation. Any deliberate violence upon anything worthy of the name of art we deem to be an act of desecration, or something analogous to it. For the same reason, those who are aesthetically cultivated frequently consider the use of improper materials, the rejection of classical principles, the attempt to create "contrived contrast," and so forth, not merely as an expression of a different taste, but rather as an assault on something like a divine order.

One may argue that sacred art becomes pious art, or perhaps even profane art, by merely changing its setting, for by so doing the end to which it is ordered necessarily changes. Gilson appears to make this very case:

> The countless representations of Christ, of the Virgin and of the saints that crowd our art galleries are just as innocent of religious meaning as any Greek or Roman divinity. When a picture is removed from a church and placed in some museum of fine arts, it does not remain the same, because it ceases to fulfil the same functions, to address itself to the same public and to aim at achieving the same end.[45]

It is not altogether obvious that Gilson is correct here. If we compare Albrecht Dürer's *Saint Sebastian Tied to a Tree* to

[45] Etienne Gilson, *The Arts of the Beautiful* (n.p.: Dalkey Archive Press, 2000), 167–68.

Piero del Pollaiolo's *Martyrdom of Saint Sebastian*, they respectively require something very different on the part of the audience, whatever their setting (both are in public galleries). The former invites the viewer to meditate on the death of St. Sebastian, whereas the latter invites the viewer to contemplate the glory of martyrdom; the former invites one into a story, the latter raises one to a theological mystery. They clearly have distinct self-contained ends. Nevertheless, even if we were to agree with Gilson that the character of sacred art is radically altered—so as no longer to be sacred at all—merely by a change of setting, I would still hold that this is not because all art really has nothing to do with religion. Rather, all art—including profane art—is precisely *religious* in the sense I now specify.

Aristotle observes the following:

> A picture painted on a panel is at once a picture and a likeness: that is, while one and the same, it is both of these, although the *being* of both is not the same, and one may contemplate it either as a picture, or as a likeness.[46]

Adopting this idea, we can say that in one sense the arts of the beautiful are ends in themselves, in that they do not belong to the servile order; but in another sense they are means, insofar as they point beyond themselves to that which they represent, and from which they derive their meaning. Art, then, can be understood as a mediator between one who is subject to it and that which it represents, in order that by it the latter may be better seized by the mind of the former. To see a lily is quite a different thing from seeing Monet's lilies, and to con-

---

[46] Quoted in ibid., 169.

template lilies having contemplated Monet's lilies is yet another thing, and yet each apprehension is, according to the wider ontology being advanced in these pages, a further ascent of the created mind into the divine mind.

The artist ascends to the mind of God, in order to incarnate his apprehension in the world, and he aims at taking his audience with him. In this way, as I have said, artists and philosophers are alike; however they are not only seekers of God, but imitators of God too. The philosopher imitates God in the possession of wisdom; the artist is an imitator of God in his creative act, for "while human art-making is clearly not a matter of strict creation, it is more properly conceived of as generation than as modification."[47] Just as there is for the philosopher, there is also a tradition spanning the world of seeing the artist as someone somewhat other-worldly, or mystical, like the priest or shaman. It is plausible that some professional artists ride on the back of this inherited notion, using it to justify work of little merit, and employing it to posit that their critics have simply failed to understand their output. However, there is a great difference between the mystical and the mystifying; the former seeks insight, clarity, and order; the latter gives rise to blindness, confusion, and chaos.

There are various reasons, then, why one might argue that all art is essentially religious. However, the reason most directly related to the wider ontology we have advanced is that the artist has as his object the deepest meaning of the world. The artist, knowingly or not, traces the twofold exemplarism which accounts for all of created reality, and incarnates his apprehension in the world. If this view is true,

---

[47] John Haldane, *An Intelligent Person's Guide to Religion* (London: Duckworth Overlook, 2005), 164.

119

then it explains why many would intuit a deep connection between art and religion, and more broadly, the aesthetic experience and the religious experience.

Not everything in the world is sacred, nor could it be (sacred implying "set apart"), but, according to the ontology defended in this thesis, everything is religious, and art is no exception. Insofar as something exemplifies the divine mind or the divine nature it is inherently religious, and since all finite beings exemplify God in such a way, all created reality is religious. Art is unique in the world however, for via the imposed form the artist adds onto finite being a human intentionality in ordering the mind of the one subject to his work toward the same ascent which he himself has undertaken. The artist *is* that part of the universe which incarnates, by the imposition on matter of a new form, that which can be grasped only by a rational nature, and by so doing causes the matter to partake of his rationality by being in a way infused with it. Art, then, becomes a type of communication, in which this extrinsic finite inanimate being is assumed into the act of conveying a truth seized in a rational nature; or rather the truth seized overflows in a dynamic act of expression into the world, being received by the work. This work conveys the object of the artist's contemplation at a depth to which conversation alone cannot attain. The artist's audience unites itself to the work, bringing its own dynamism to it, and thereby shares in the artist's ascent to the uncreated reality—known via the world around him—denoted by the work.

One may object, how can *bad* art be religious? The answer is that bad art is religious in the same way as bad religion is religious, like that of devil-worshippers. A blasphemy, or sacrilege, is still a religious act, for such an act derives its meaning from its object, namely God. Indeed, bad art—as I have argued above—is akin to blasphemy; it is like an assault on a divine order. It is commonly noted that there is a more pronounced tendency for bad art to emerge in cultures that are desacralized and hostile to religion; if this is true, the ontology presented here provides a plausible explanation. In turn, many contemporary pieces, issued by people who would reject the view of art and the artist which I have advanced, mark a deliberate departure not only from beauty, but also from unity, truth, goodness, nobility, and so forth. In such productions there is a chosen privation of the transcendental attributes together, opted for in a single act of desecration, or something akin to it.[48] All art, then, is religious. The ability of the theocentric ontology defended by my position to explain this fact is an advantage, given the widespread intuition that art and religion are closely related; it may also be capable of offering robust support to the sense widely felt that art in the Western tradition has lost its way.

---

[48] Obvious examples of this are the productions of the Chapman Brothers, Tracey Emin, Sarah Lucas, and Gavin Turk, among many other fakes in the "art business"; generally "expressionistic dance" and "musical serialism" may be criticized along the same lines.

Conclusion

I learned both what is secret and what is manifest, for
wisdom, the fashioner of all things, taught me.
—The Wisdom of Solomon 7:22

M Y OVERALL INTENTION for this book has been to
demonstrate that the common reading of Aquinas
as a pure—albeit Christian—Aristotelian is profoundly insensitive to the central Platonic elements in his
thought. It has been necessary therefore to show that the way
modern philosophers have largely understood the metaphysics of Aquinas—as a choice of Aristotle over Plato—is a misunderstanding which arose due to a particular reading of him
emerging with the nineteenth-century Thomistic revival.
This I have called the narrative of discontinuity. In contrast to
this I have argued that Aquinas's ontology constitutes a much
richer synthesis of both Aristotelian and Platonic metaphysics. He ought therefore to be understood as having achieved
something much greater than is generally thought, namely
the bringing together of the two predominant Hellenistic
currents, often judged to be irreconcilable, and issuing forth
in a single coherent ontology.

I had first to show that the mistaken reading was the domi-
nant one, and therefore give numerous examples of popular
authors, historians, philosophers and theologians failing to
recognize the true character of Aquinas's ontology as a synthesis of Platonic and Aristotelian metaphysics. Then I had to
demonstrate how such a synthesis emerged, arising from the
most ancient philosophical questions concerning the nature

of the finite and the infinite, which in turn gave rise to the problem known as that of the one and the many.

Aquinas's own ontology is not presented by him in a single argument, being rather the fundamental structure on which sits everything he writes. I have nevertheless attempted to present this ontology, referred to in a scattered fashion through Thomas's works, as a coherent worldview, and in so doing I have brought together many of the more apposite primary texts and drawn on the insights of those who have worked in this area.

As Aquinas himself does not give sufficient terminology for such a task, the "first wave" of scholars had to invent terminology, and were found to disagree about the proper interpretation of Aquinas. Therefore, I undertook an assessment of the terms of both Fabro and Geiger, and how the later North Americans, especially Wippel and Doolan, have sought to reconcile differences. This enabled me to further illustrate how the "participationists" to a lesser or greater degree inadvertently—and in the case of Clarke, absolutely purposely—launched an assault on the entire narrative of discontinuity, i.e., the received view of Thomas' relation to previous, non-Aristotelian philosophy.

Having accomplished this in the first two chapters, I had yet to display the view of the world which follows from such a Platonic and Aristotelian synthesis. The first two chapters brought us to how Thomistic participation metaphysics gives rise to a theory of divine exemplarism, and from this I presented Aquinas's account of creation as an "icon of God," and analyzed the various analogies employed to convey such a worldview. For completeness, I had still to consider the Five Ways, which are generally—and not wholly correctly, in my view—considered by many as a presentation of Aquinas's own natural theology, in order to situate them properly in his wider thought.

In the final chapter I considered how the narrative of discontinuity has affected our understanding of Aquinas in relation to other periods of history, especially the Renaissance; also how the enormous output of material culture during the Renaissance, considered by many a high point in European history, may be linked in part precisely to the reception of Aquinas's ontology. This naturally took me into the area of aesthetics, in which I demonstrated that Aquinas was an heir to a Platonic theory of aesthetics—which was itself linked to the development of Gothic architecture that emerged in the preceding century—and which Thomas then developed. That Aquinas's ontology could accommodate the Platonic aesthetics so widely felt to be attractive, and that—being a totally theocentric ontology—it could account for the widely felt intuition that there was some profound relationship between the aesthetic and religious experiences, I argued was of philosophical advantage. An effect of advancing such a case was the drawing out of a theory of vocation concerning the artist and the philosopher, their difference and their complementarity, in pursuing truth, indeed *the* Truth.

This is a work primarily of metaphysics, with considerations of epistemology and, later, aesthetics and philosophy of religion as supporting features. However, my own hope throughout has been that we might see anew the tradition of the Schoolmen as one of enduring principles, though always renewed, refined, and newly applied, rather than a mere sequence of ruptures down the centuries, at the end of which we find ourselves still stumbling in the dark. Indeed, one might be inclined to say that this entire work has had as its underlying purpose from the outset to share in the assault on the narrative of discontinuity.

I wish to make one more point, with which I will conclude, which concerns the philosophy of religion. The ontology I have advanced, and which I claim is Aquinas's own, leads to the discovery of God only via the discovery of the world as an *icon* of him. That is, we discover *that* God exists, and also that the world conveys something of his inner life, simply by the world being the thing it is. However, as we have said, this can be likened to a portrait, or a piece of music about someone, or a spoken description of someone. To know something *about* a person differs radically in kind from knowing him. We discover, then, an *icon* of the one who is the explanation of all that is, and yet have no way of actually knowing him directly. It is plausible, I suggest, that it is out of this sense of alienation from the maker of the cosmos that a longing for some encounter with the divine arises, and hence a *natural religion*, with as many manifestations as human communities, seeking without success to bridge the infinite void between creature and Creator. It is impossible; we cannot go beyond a world of which we ourselves are a part. The only alternative would be for the Creator Himself to bridge the void by somehow entering the world, by being part of the world and yet remaining God, a *synthesis* of both. Looking upon such a living synthesis we may no longer see only a mere image, but behold him face to face, so that he might say to us, "he who has seen me has seen the Father" of the world (John 14:9). In turn, the ontology advanced in this book would cohere well with an *incarnation story* to assume and succeed it, so that it may become part of the repertoire of the theologian. It is, therefore, a fitting *praeambula fidei*:

Conclusion

It is obvious that the phrase "preambles of faith" is one devised and used from the side of belief; it is the believer who compares truths about God that he holds only thanks to the grace of faith and those truths about God that philosophers came to know by way of demonstrative proof. But what is referred to by the phrase is precisely those philosophically established truths about God. Looking at the sum of revealed truths, the theologian will notice the subset he calls preambles and he will distinguish them from the mysteries of faith. Only the latter belong to faith *per se*: there is no other way to hold them as true in this life. But along with the revelation of the mysteries, that is, those truths about God that would not be known apart from God revealing them—for example, the Trinity of persons—believers are given as well the truths that the philosophers have proved. Implicit in the mysteries is of course the truth that God exists and that he is one and intelligent and the like.[1]

It is plausible that the worldview that follows from the ontology advanced here needs, as it were, to be "completed" by an *incarnation story*, bridging the infinite creature-Creator void; a narrative of God entering the world—entering history—not just for a time, but to remain until the conclusion of the world. Aquinas himself believed in such a narrative. He believed that God had indeed become flesh, possessing a created human nature and an uncreated divine nature in a single personhood. This incarnation would be perpetuated under the Eucharistic Presence until the world's conclusion.

[1] Ralph McInerny, *Praeambula Fidei: Thomism and the God of Philosophers* (Washington: Catholic University of America Press, 2006), 30–31.

I judge therefore that it is of particular philosophical advantage that the ontology expounded herein not only accommodates such a story, deeply believed by its original proponent, but appears to meet it so fittingly.

Bibliography

The Holy Bible, Revised Standard Version: Second Catholic Edition. San Francisco: Ignatius Press, 2006.

Aquinas, Thomas. *An Exposition of the "On the Hebdomads" of Boethius.* Translated by Janice L. Schultz and Edward A. Synan. Washington: Catholic University of America Press, 2001.

——— *Commentary on Aristotle's Metaphysics.* Translated by John P. Rowan. [n.p.] Dumb Ox Books, 1995.

——— *Commentary on Aristotle's Physics.* Translated by Richard J. Blackwell, Richard J. Spath, and W. Edmund Thirkel. London: Routledge and Kegan Paul, 1963.

——— *Commentary on the Liber de Causis.* Translated by Vincent A. Guagliardo, O.P., Charles R. Hess, O.P., and Richard C. Taylor. Washington: Catholic University of America Press, 1996.

——— *Commentary on the Sentences*, https://aquinas.cc

——— *Compendium of Theology.* Translated by Richard J. Regan. New York: Oxford University Press, 2009.

——— *Disputed Questions on Spiritual Creatures.* Translated by Mary C. Fitzpatrick and John J. Wellmuth. Milwaukee: Marquette University Press, 1949.

——— *In librum B. Dionysii De divinis nominibus expositio*, http://www.corpusthomisticum.org/cdn01.html

——— *On Being and Essence.* Translated by Armand Maurer.

Toronto: Pontifical Institute of Mediaeval Studies, 1968.

—— *Quaestiones de quodlibet*. Leuven: Leuven University Press, 1987.

—— *Quaestiones Disputatae De Potentia Dei*. Translated by the English Dominican Fathers. Westminster, MD: The Newman Press, 1952.

—— *Questiones Disputatae de Veritate*. Translated by Robert W. Mulligan, S. J. Chicago: Henry Regnery Company, 1952.

—— *Summa Contra Gentiles*. Translated by Anton C. Pegis. Indiana: University of Notre Dame Press, 1976.

—— *Summa Theologica*. New York: Benziger Bros., 1948.

Aristotle, *The Complete Works of Aristotle: The Revised Oxford Translation* (2 volumes), Jonathan Barnes, ed. Chichester: Princeton University Press, 1984.

Augustine of Hippo. *Of True Religion*. Translated by J. H. S. Burleigh. Chicago: Henry Regnery Company, 1959.

Beardsley, Monroe C. *Aesthetics: Problems in the Philosophy of Criticism*, 2nd edition. Indianapolis: Hackett Publishing Company, Inc., 1981.

Cavanagh, O.P., Pius. *Life of St. Thomas Aquinas*. London: Burns & Oates, 1890.

Chesterton, G. K. *Saint Thomas Aquinas*. New York: Doubleday, 2001.

Chidester, David. *Christianity*. London: Penguin Books, 2001.

Clarke, S. J., W. Norris. *Explorations in Metaphysics*. Indiana: University of Notre Dame Press, 1994.

—— *The One and the Many*. Indiana: University of Notre Dame Press, 2001.

———— *The Philosophical Approach to God*. New York: Fordham University Press, 2007.

Copenhaver, Brian P. & Charles B. Schmitt. *Renaissance Philosophy*. Oxford: Oxford University Press, 2002.

Copleston, S.J., Frederick. *Aquinas*. London: Penguin Books, 1991.

Cross, Richard. *The Medieval Christian Philosophers: An Introduction*. London: I.B. Tauris, 2014.

Curtright, Travis, ed. *Thomas More: Why Patron of Statesmen?*. New York: Lexington Books, 2015.

D'Arcy, S.J., M.C. *St. Thomas Aquinas*. London: Burns & Oates, 1953.

Dawkins, Richard. *The God Delusion*. London: Transworld Publishers, 2007.

Dezza, S.J., Paulo. *Metaphysica Generalis*. Rome: [n.p.] 1945.

Doolan, Gregory T. *Aquinas on the Divine Ideas as Exemplar Causes*. Washington: Catholic University of America Press, 2008.

Dionysius the Areopagite (Pseudo-Dionysius). *The Divine Names*. Translated by C.E. Holt. London: [n.p.] 1920.

Eco, Umberto. *Art and Beauty in the Middle Ages*. London: Yale University Press, 1986.

Eliot, T.S. *Notes Towards the Definition of Culture*. London: Faber and Faber, 1962.

Fabro, C.P.S., Cornelio. *La nozione metafisica di partecipazione*, 2nd edition. Turin: Società Editrice Internazionale, 1963.

———— "The Intensive Hermeneutics of Thomistic Philosophy: The Notion of Participation." *Review of Metaphysics* 27.3:

Commemorative Issue Thomas Aquinas 1224–1274, 1974.

Feser, Edward. *Aquinas*. London: Oneworld Publications, 2009.

——— *Scholastic Metaphysics: A Contemporary Introduction*. Lancaster: Gazelle Books, 2014.

Freeman, Kathleen. *Ancilla to the Pre-Socratics*. Cambridge, MA: Harvard University Press, 1948.

Garrigou-Lagrange, O.P., Reginald. *Reality: A Synthesis of Thomistic Thought*. St. Louis: Herder, 1950.

Gaut, Berys and Dominic McIver Lopes, eds. *The Routledge Companion to Aesthetics*, 2nd edition. London: Routledge, 2005.

Geiger, O.P., Louis-Bertrand. *La participation dans la philosophie de s. Thomas d'Aquin*, 2nd edition. Paris: Librairie Philosophique J. Vrin, 1953.

Giacon, Carlo. *Atto e Potenza*. Brescia: [n.p.] 1947.

Gilson, Etienne. *The Arts of the Beautiful*. Dalkey Archive Press, 2000.

——— *The Christian Philosophy of St. Thomas Aquinas*. Indiana: University of Notre Dame Press, 1994.

Haldane, John. *An Intelligent Person's Guide to Religion*. London: Duckworth Overlook, 2005.

Honderich, Ted, ed. *The Oxford Companion to Philosophy*. New York: Oxford University Press, 1995.

Hughes, Philip. *A History of the Church*. London: Sheed & Ward, 1948.

Kenny, Anthony. *Aquinas*. Oxford: Oxford University Press,

1980.

——— *A New History of Western Philosophy*. Oxford: Oxford University Press, 2010.

Kristeller, Paul Oskar. *Medieval Aspects of Renaissance Learning*. Duke University Press, 1974.

Luscombe, David. *Medieval Thought*. Oxford: Oxford University Press, 1997.

Maritain, Jacques. *Art and Scholasticism*. London: Sheed and Ward, 1930.

McInerny, Ralph. *Praeambula Fidei: Thomism and the God of Philosophers*. Washington: Catholic University of America Press, 2006.

More, Thomas. *The Complete Works of St. Thomas More*, John Guy, Ralph Keen, Clarence Miller, and Ruth McGugan, eds. New Haven: Yale University Press, 1997.

——— *Dialogue Concerning Heresies*. New York: Scepter Publishers, 2006.

Nolan, Daniel, "Hyperintensional Metaphysics." In *Philosophical Studies: An International Journal for Philosophy in the Analytic Tradition*, Vol. 171, No. 1, Special Issue: Selected Papers from the American Philosophical Association, Pacific Division, 2013 Meeting, October 2014.

Origen, *On First Principles*. Translated by John Behr. Oxford: Oxford University Press, 2017.

O'Sullivan, Richard, ed. *The King's Good Servant: Papers Read to the Thomas More Society of London*. Oxford: Basil Blackwell, 1941.

Owens, Joseph. *The Doctrine of Being in the Aristotelian Meta-*

physics. Toronto: Pontifical Institute of Mediaeval Studies, 1951.

Panofsky, Erwin. *On the Abbey Church of St.-Denis and its Art Treasures.* Princeton: Princeton University Press, 1979.

Pater, Walter. *Studies in the History of the Renaissance.* Oxford: Oxford University Press, 1986.

Pieper, Josef. *Guide to Thomas Aquinas.* San Francisco: Ignatius Press, 1991.

Plato, *Philebus.* Translated by Dorothea Frede. Indianapolis: Hackett Publishing Company, 1993.

—— *Plato: Complete Works*, John M. Cooper, ed. Indianapolis: Hackett Publishing Company, 1997.

Plotinus, *The Enneads.* Translated by Stephen Mackenna. London: Faber and Faber, 1956.

Rex, Richard. *The Theology of John Fisher.* Cambridge: Cambridge University Press, 2003.

Russell, Bertrand. *History of Western Philosophy.* London: Routledge, 1995.

Scruton, Roger. *Beauty.* Oxford: Oxford University Press, 2009.

—— *An Intelligent Person's Guide to Modern Culture.* South Bend, IN: St. Augustine's Press, 2000.

Sire, Henry. *Phoenix from the Ashes.* Kettering, Ohio: Angelico Press, 2015.

Sturz, S.J., Edward. *The Works and Days of John Fisher.* Cambridge: Harvard University Press, 1967.

Tatarkiewicz, W., *Medieval Aesthetics.* Translated R. M. Montgomery. The Hague: Mouton, 1970.

Bibliography

Tolkien, J. R. R. *The Silmarillion*. Boston: Houghton Mifflin Company, 1977.

Towey, Anthony. *An Introduction to Christian Theology*. London: Bloomsbury T&T Clark, 2013.

Tyndale, William. *The Obedience of the Christian Man*. Clermont-Ferrand: Digireads, 2012.

Urmson, J. O. and Jonathan Rée, eds. *The Concise Encyclopedia of Western Philosophy & Philosophers*. London: Routledge, 1993.

Wippel, John F. *The Metaphysical Thought of Thomas Aquinas*. Washington: Catholic University of America Press, 2000.

Index of Names

About the Author

SEBASTIAN MORELLO was trained in philosophy by Sir Roger Scruton and Andrew Pinsent. He is a lecturer, columnist, and popular public speaker in the United Kingdom and throughout Europe. Morello has previously co-authored books on subjects of philosophy and education. He lives in Bedfordshire, England, with his wife and children.

Printed in Great Britain
by Amazon

57209429R00088